The Picture of My Early Life

(*Jibansmriti*)

Tagore on frontpage

Also read:

Tagore's Best Short Stories

ISBN: 978 81 908841 5 0

The Picture of My Early Life
(*Jibansmriti*)

Rabindranath Tagore

Translatation: Prasenjit Saha

With an Introduction by Patrick Colm Hogan

frontpage

frontpage
www.frontpagepublications.com

First published 2013

Frontpage Publications Limited
Level 2, 13 John Prince's Street, London W1G 0JR, United Kingdom

Frontpage
Level 6, Constantia, 11 Dr U N Brahmachari Sarani, Kolkata 700017, India

British Library Cataloguing in Publication Data
A catalogue record for this book is available from the British Library

ISBN: 978 93 810430 7 3

Printed in India
by Sadhana Press Private Limited
76 B B Ganguli Street, Kolkata 700012

Typeset by Compuset International
85 Park Street, Kolkata 700016

Reading *Jibansmriti* (The Picture of My Early Life) One-Hundred Years Later

TAGORE BEGINS HIS *Jibansmriti* with an extended analogy. Memories are not a documentary record of the past, an objective history of necessary facts in the necessary order. They are something much more fragmentary and personal. They are like paintings, moments partially isolated in time. It is as if, due to their emotional intensity, an artist had selected them from the rush of experience. The idea recalls Tagore's own paintings, most obviously the haunting figures of young women – their eyes both desolate and proud, as if concealing a despair that nonetheless seeps out from the lines and colours of the flat surface.

If anyone should need evidence that Tagore knew what he was saying, there is ample support in current research on memory and the human brain. But, for the reader of Tagore's reminiscences, the key thing here is probably not the scientific accuracy of the observation. It is, rather, the artistic use to which Tagore puts this observation.

There are many reasons one might read Tagore's memoir. The life of a distinguished public figure is intrinsically interesting. Moreover, Rabindranath was not the only person of historical importance among the Tagores. They were a family of almost unparalleled distinction. They recall the Brontes, the James's (William, Henry, and Alice), the Bachs, but go beyond even these in the breadth of their accomplishments. Then there was the circle of their acquaintances, which included such cultural giants as the novelist Bankim Chandra Chattopadhyay and the scholar Ishwar Chandra Vidyasagar. Further, the Tagores were deeply involved with the major cultural and political developments of the period. Reading *Jibansmriti* can give one a deeper sense of what it was like to live in such a context.

These and other reasons for picking up Tagore's book are certainly right. Yet, the greatest value of the book is perhaps suggested in that opening image, the metaphor of the mind's painter sketching out the momentary experiences of grief or delight, then elaborating them into enduring memories – true more to the personal experience of the artist than to the facts. Specifically, Tagore's reminiscences are themselves simultaneously a work of art and a great source for understanding Tagore's artistic creativity elsewhere.

Jibansmriti as Literature

As a work of art in itself, the book includes many of the properties that characterise Tagore's fiction and poetry. We may roughly divide the structure of the book into three parts. The opening sections treat Tagore's early childhood. These take up some of Tagore's most enduring and affecting concerns. They partially express the tenderness for childhood that is so characteristic of his other writings. Indeed, perhaps the most pervasive feeling in Tagore's literary works in what the Sanskrit theorists called *vatsalya* and current writers on emotion refer to as 'attachment'. This is, first of all, the bonding of parents with young children. But it extends to the bonding of lovers and close friends. Related to this, the most important source of pathos in Tagore's writings is the result of broken attachments – rejection, separation, bereavement.

On the other hand, speaking of his own case, Tagore does not dwell on either vatsalya, attachment or frustration. Indeed, Tagore's attitude towards his early self is decidedly critical. At the same time, he is forgiving of his childhood faults and errors. This leads to a second aspect of his treatment of childhood. One of Tagore's recurring concerns throughout his writings is freedom. He is repulsed and angered by the attempts of parents and teachers to force children into fixed and rigid ways of acting and thinking. Tagore repeatedly emphasises that they need their freedom to grow intellectually and emotionally. That freedom means that they will make mistakes. But the mistakes too are necessary for growth.

The second large part of *Jibansmriti* focuses on Tagore's youth. Here, an even sharper authorial irony is aimed at the grandiloquence of adolescent poetry. Here, too, however, Tagore's criticisms are qualified by an insistence that the teenager's confident self-assertion is a good thing, a necessary condition for later development. Some of Tagore's stories take up the reverse of this condition – the debilitating results of humiliation, the ways that shame (all too easily provoked in adolescence) may result in enduring harm. A fine example of this may be found in his story, *Chutti,* where an unattractive adolescent boy is driven to tragic actions in part by his sense of shame before his family.

But, again, in treating himself, Tagore is not inclined to pathos. Thus, this second section comprises a series of engaging and witty anecdotes. Often, Tagore is the object of his own humour in these stories. At other times, his family or acquaintances come in for good-hearted chiding as well.

The third large part of *Jibansmriti* changes tone again. Rather than the critical tenderness of the childhood chapters or the irony of those concerning adolescence, this treatment of young adulthood takes up Tagore's philosophical and mystical leanings. Certainly, Tagore's religious and theological reflections are important in their own right. However, the most distinctive and affecting feature of these reflections may not be not so much what they express directly as what they suggest indirectly.

This final part of *Jibansmriti* includes the most profound expression of Tagore's own attachment feelings and the searing pain of attachment rupture. In the midst of his reflections on life and nature, Tagore turns suddenly to his mother and her early death. He then explains that this loss was soothed by the comforts of his sister-in-law. That was Kadambari Devi. She was, in effect, his new mother, and perhaps, throughout his life, the object of his deepest attachment. He goes on to explain that, having passed through the loss of his mother relatively unscarred, he had a scarring encounter with death later in his young life. That second loss was the most wrenching devastation of attachment he could experience. What is perhaps most striking about this encounter with death is that Tagore never really explains it to the reader. From other sources, we learn that this terrible event was the suicide of his beloved sister-in-law. The lack of explanation, the abstract and almost mystical way he treats this encounter with death – these are perhaps as significant as the depth of the hurt itself. They suggest the deep roots of Tagore's metaphysical thought in the very concrete experiences of love and grief.

Reminiscence and Creativity

Many writers have remarked on the importance of Kadambari Devi for Tagore's other writings. The most obvious case is the novella, *Nashtanir,* which concerns the relationship between a young man and his sister-in-law, who is neglected by her husband. But this fairly straightforward biographical connection is perhaps less interesting than the more indirect manifestations of Kadambari Devi's memory. For example, in the story *Jibita o Mrita,* Tagore recounts the life and suicide of a young woman named Kadambini. Literally, the story presents Kadambini as a living woman who is believed to be dead, is treated as if she is dead, and even for a time thinks of herself as dead. It is not difficult to see that one source of this story was the condition of the neglected sister-in-law. Kadambini's life is recognised by her family only after she has killed herself. Perhaps the same thing was true for Kadambari Devi.

The problem with Kadambari Devi's story, like many stories in real life, was that it was filled with complexity and accident. At least in one common view, art does not simply repeat life, but structures and clarifies it. Indeed, that is how art presents us with social and political themes. Tagore's transformation of Kadambari Devi's tragedy does just this by giving metaphorical resonance to the literally implausible idea that a living woman is believed to be dead. Tagore introduces Kadambini as, specifically, a widow. Altering the facts of Kadambari's life, he takes up a widespread social dilemma and gives his sister-in-law's pain a thematic point. As a widow, she is in effect treated as if she is dead. She is already as white as a ghost in her colourless robes, as inauspicious as a corpse.

In a case such as this, we begin to glimpse the processes that underlie Tagore's creativity. Here is another example. Early in *Jibansmriti,* Tagore describes his enthusiasm for writing and the notebook he used for this purpose, as well as the relation of his writing to his elder brother. This cluster of memories is one key source for the main character in *Khata*. But, once again, Tagore did not simply record his own childhood experience. He re-imagined it. Specifically, when he wrote the story, he was a successful young author, esteemed not only by family and friends, but by the great figures of Bengali literature. He could feel self-confident and, even with his sharply self-critical eye, rightly experience satisfaction in some of his accomplishments. The chain of events that led to this point began with his notebook. In this context, he thought – what if I had been a girl? What if I had the same interests, desires, capacities; what if I even had the same notebook – but was then married off at the age of nine? The result would have almost certainly been stifled capacities, perhaps even debilitating humiliation.

These are sorrowful cases. But, as the second part of *Jibansmriti* shows, Tagore was capable of developing mirth as well. His own ironic self-criticism reappears in the representation of the well-meaning but feckless philosopher, Taraprasanna, in *Taraprassaner Kirti*. Taraprasanna writes a book on Vedanta in order to make money for his daughters' dowries. However, it proves so thoroughly incomprehensible that no one buys the book. The commercial failure of Taraprasanna's book parallels the commercial failure of Tagore's first book. Here Tagore again transforms his experience. Taraprasanna is not an adolescent, but an adult who should have outgrown the teenage excesses that characterised Tagore's youthful writings. That transformation is part of what makes the character comic. Moreover, the transformation is consequential in other ways. Taraprasanna's opacity contributes to Tagore's criticism of pretence and obscurantism in philosophical work – work that should contribute to people's spiritual self-understanding through its own lucidity.

In these cases, then, we see Tagore doing two things. First, his transformative re-imagination of the biographical material intensifies its emotional force, tragic or comic. Second, that re-imagination relocates the biographical material in a context that gives it broader social significance. Moreover, in each case, we see that Tagore exhibits an exceptional capacity for what is called 'effortful perspective taking'. This is the process of putting oneself in the place of another person. Perspective taking is more successful to the extent that one can incorporate the particularities of the other person. This becomes increasingly difficult and consequential to the extent that one's own properties are different from the other person's – as when Tagore imagines himself in the place of people whose sex or age or class is different from his own.

Stepping Outside the Chalk Circle

These are not the only ways that Tagore transforms his biographical sources through imagination. Moreover, such transformations are not the only ways in which *Jibansmriti* contributes to our understanding of Tagore's creativity. In keeping with current creativity research, *Jibansmriti* shows the extent to which Tagore's background was extremely rich, including a wide range of arts and sciences, as well as both Indian and European traditions. Far from being confined to the narrow circle of his own place and time, Tagore's mind wandered freely across continents and centuries. That breadth was a constant source for innovation.

The mention of a narrow circle recalls Tagore's memory of being confined as a child in a circle of chalk. This confinement serves as an image of everything life – particularly the life of children – should *not* be. The chalk circle is rigorous obedience and discipline. It is the opposite of play. The freedom of play is just what risks mistakes, but at the same time allows the full development of creativity. Indeed, one could argue that Tagore's opposition to that narrow circle of chalk was the single most important impulse in his artistic development. One urge underlying all his creative work was the desire to play, to jostle ideas, images, and feelings without a predetermined commitment to some specific result; to allow half-formed notions to engage with strange fancies and lead to curious outcomes. Those outcomes may be failures, or they may be great successes. But they will not be ordinary.

Indeed, that is not all the chalk circle suggests in this context. It was, explicitly, the line drawn by Lakshmana around Sita. This has many implications. Perhaps the most important for us is that Tagore's story locates him, not in the place of the warrior king Rama, but in the place of an exiled girl and an abandoned woman – Sita, whose story is centrally a story of broken attachment. Even as a child, it seems, Tagore was imagining himself into what he was not.

This leads us to a final value of reading *Jibansmriti*. No one who picks up this English translation was born, like Tagore, in colonial Bengal 150 years ago. Relatively few are Bengali speakers. Few are novelists or poets, painters or composers of music. Only some have anything like Tagore's philosophical and literary background. In short, we are all different from Tagore in many important ways. *Jibansmriti* not only allows us to infer some aspects of Tagore's re-imagined life experiences. It also invites us, in some small measure, to share those experiences, to engage in the perspective taking that seems to have come so easily to Tagore, to broaden our own thought and feeling by incorporating aspects of his. Indeed, this is perhaps the most important value of reading Tagore's reminiscences. It is the value that encompasses and gives personal meaning to all the others.

25 December 2012 — Patrick Colm Hogan

Translator's note

TRANSLATING *JIBANSMRITI* WAS a challenge and a pleasure too. I have tried to be as true to the original as possible, in content, form and style. Certain words have not been translated on purpose, and most of these have been italicised. In several cases, the meanings have been clarified within the text. As for the rest, I will try to offer simple contextual explanations here. Further details, for those interested, are readily available on the internet, specifically Wikipedia.

Terms for relationships in Bengali are complex. *Dada* is the term for elder brother, *didi* for elder sister; bor-dada, mej-dada, sej-dada, bor-didi and chor-didi stand for eldest brother, second-eldest brother, third-eldest brother, eldest sister and youngest of the elder sisters respectively. *Dada* can also be affixed to a name, like Guna-dada. Honorifics with names can be a prefix like *Srijukta*, or suffixes like *Mahasay* (commonly *mosai*), *babu* and *-ji*. Thus *mastermosai* is a teacher, *panditmosai* is a priest and *munshi-ji* is a clerk. *Sahib* is a term originally used to denote a westerner. Certain very specific terms have been used in the text: *Tarkaratna* or *Tarkachudamani* is an expert in debates, *Tattaratna* is a repository of knowledge, *Vendantabagis* is an expert on the scriptures and *Bachaspati* is an acclaimed orator. *Kabi* is a poet whereas *Kathak* is a raconteur.

The great Indian epics, *Ramayana* and *Mahabharata* find many references. The original Sanskrit version of the *Ramayana* is ascribed to the *Maharshi* (great sage) Balmiki; several other versions are mentioned: *Uttarramacharita* and Krittibas' version. King Dasarath of Ayodhya is the father of Rama. The version of

Mahabharata by Kasiramdas finds a mention; Bhisma is the grand patriarch of the *Kaurava* clan in the *Mahabharata*, while Bhima and Arjuna are two of the five heroic brothers of the *Pandava* clan. Several ancient and medieval Sanskrit poets are referred, like Vidyapati, Chandidas, Bopdeb, Bhababhuti and Jayadeva. A *sloka* is a Sanskrit verse. *Meghdoot* or The Heavenly Messenger, *Kumarsambhava* or The Birth of Kumar and *Shakuntala* are the works of *Kalidasa*, acknowledged as the greatest poet and dramatist in Sanskrit, who lived in the 5th century AD. Amaru wrote *Amaru-sataka*, or The Hundred Verses. *Geet Govind* or The Song of Govinda (Krishna) was written by the 12th century poet Jayadeva. Michael Mauhusudhan Dutt, the 18th century poet who originally wrote in English before switching to his mother tongue, is the author of *Meghnadbadh Kavya*, or the Ballad of the Slaying of Meghnad.

Brahmins are the priestly caste at the top of the traditional social hierarchy. *Upanayanaya* ceremony is the coming-of-age ceremony where young boys from the uppermost caste acquire the sacred thread and are taught the *Gayatri Mantra*, which is a revered verse from The Rig Veda and then they become complete Brahmins. *Bramhosamaj* was a society that arose from the religious reformation movement started by Debendranath Tagore and Raja Ram Mohun Roy in the 1830s. The followers were known as *Brahmos*. *Vaishnava* is a form of *Bhakti* (intense devotion) movement that arose in medieval India. It gave rise to lyrical poetry not only in Sanskrit, but also in other dialects. *Mythili* is one such dialect. *Padabali* is a collection of *Vaishnava* songs.

Saraswati is the Goddess of Learning and Arts in the Hindu pantheon. *Maheswar* is another name for Lord Shiva while *Shyama* is a form of Goddess Kali. *Hari, Shyam* and *Braja* are other names of Lord Krishna, while *Nandarani* is Krishna's mother. *Yama* is the God of Death. *Ganesha,* or the elephant-headed God, is 'The Remover of Obstacles' and is invoked at the beginning of any auspicious event. *Lakshmi* is the Goddess of Wealth. *Yaksha* is a benevolent nature-spirit.

Raga and the feminine form, *ragini,* are the combination of notes that form the framework of Indian classical music, both Hindustani and Carnatic. *Raga Bhairavi, Raga Purabi, Raga Jogia,*

Raga Kafi, Dipak Ragini and *Behag Ragini* appear in the text. *Tala* is the underlying rhythm in classical music. *Tappa* is a form of semi-classical music, said to have originated as the song of the camel drivers. *Bauls* are itinerant minstrels of Bengal, renowned for their folk music and an egalitarian world view. *Kirtans* are devotional folk songs. *Tillana* is a rhythmic piece in Carnatic music. *Bramhasangeet* is a form of devotional music of the *Bramhos,* dedicated to *Bramha,* The Creator. *Shehnai* is a wind instrument traditionally played at weddings. *Veena* is a stringed instrument and can be of several types. *Tanpura* is also a stringed drone instrument while *tabla* consists of a left and a right drum.

Sandesh is a sweet made out of cottage cheese. *Gamcha* is a thin woven towel. A *ghat* refers to a paved bank of a pond or a river, usually with steps leading down to the water. *Dak-bunglows* were set up during the British period for use by the postal service, but later these were used as government rest houses. Lastly, a *teapoy* is a three-legged table common during the British period.

2 October 2012 Prasenjit Saha

Prologue

I DO NOT KNOW who etches the pictures on the canvas of our memory. Whosoever does it, these are pictures that are drawn. With paint brush in hand, he does not sit down only to reproduce whatever happens in front of him. He adds and deletes scenes in accordance with his taste. Big incidents can be reduced to smaller episodes while small ones can be made bigger. He does not hesitate to alter the sequence of events by bringing forward later events and pushing the initial ones back. He does all these since his job is primarily to draw pictures and not record history.

In this way, the sequence of events in life goes on, on the outside; while on the inside, pictures are being painted. Both are interrelated, but are not the same happenings.

We do not get the opportunity to view our inner canvas in its entirety. We glance at a picture or two now and then. Most of it lies in darkness, unremembered. But the artist paints continuously – who knows why he paints, or when he will finish, or, when complete, which gallery would display the pictures.

A few years ago, when someone asked me to describe incidents from my past life, I entered the room with the drawings, to gather the information. I thought I would be satisfied with collecting details of a few past events in my life. But when I opened the door, I realised that my reminiscences did not constitute factual life history – rather, these were the creations of some invisible artist. The displayed colours in many places were not reflected images of the outside world – the colours were from the artist's personal palette that he had had to mix with his own feelings; thus the impressions on the canvas of the mind cannot be used as evidence in a court of law.

In this storehouse of memories, it may be impossible to collect proper historical facts, but viewing pictures can be addictive and I was afflicted by this addiction. When a traveller travels along a path or seeks shelter in a wayside inn, the path he travels on or the inn he rests in are not pictures of the mind; at that stage, these are immediate necessities that are very real. When the needs are satisfied and the traveller has moved on, only then can these be viewed as pictures. When one looks back at all the towns and countryside, rivers and mountains travelled through at the dawn of life, while crossing the threshold of the rest house at the end of the day, then in the fading light after sunset, all these scenes appear as a picture. When I had an opportunity to turn back to look at the picture, just one look made my mind completely engrossed in what I beheld.

Was the curiosity that developed in my mind due only to a natural attachment towards incidents in my past life? Of course, there is always some attachment, but a picture has its own attraction solely as a picture. The statement in the first chapter of *Uttarramcharita*, that the pictures that Lakshman presented before Sita for her amusement charmed her because there was a connection with her past life, is not fully true.

There is nothing at all in these memoirs that qualifies to be made memorable forever. Literature is not solely dependent on the respect for the subject matter; rather, if I can render what I have experienced well in such a fashion that it can also be experienced by the reader, only then will he love and respect that literature. If one can effectively express in words, the image that is etched as a picture in one's memory, only then can it qualify for a place in the ranks of literature.

Thus, these pictures from my memory form a literary collection. It would be wrong to consider this as a detailed account of my life. In that respect, this composition is far from complete and is extremely redundant.

The Beginning of My Education

WE WERE THREE boys growing up together. My companions were elder to me by two years. When they started getting their lessons from our teacher, my education also commenced, though I have no recollection of the starting point.

I can only remember, *'jal pore, pata nare* – rain drops fall, making leaves quiver'. At that moment, I had just managed to overcome the storm of mastering difficult spellings and to keep afloat. I read on that day, *'jal pore, pata nare'*. This was perhaps the first piece of poetry in my life. When I recollect the euphoria of that day, I can well understand why rhyme is so essential to poetry. Since there is rhyme, poetry does not seem to end with the words – even when the message is over, the rhythm does not end but carries on playing in the mind through the faculty of hearing. In this manner, the rhythm in the words of the rhyme I had learnt that day kept repeating itself over and over again in my mind, dominating my whole consciousness with falling rain drops and quivering leaves.

Another incident from my childhood has stuck to my memory. We used to have a helping hand named Kailas Mukherjee who had been serving us for many, many years. He was almost like a member of the family. He was extremely witty. He was always joking and laughing with everyone. He would embarrass newly wedded grooms in the family with his derisive jokes. People said that his ability to raise a laugh did not diminish even after his death. There was a time when the elders in my family tried to communicate with spirits using a planchet. One day, Kailas Mukherjee's name appeared scribbled on their planchet. He was asked, "Well, can you inform us about the condition of the place you are in presently?" The reply came back, "What I learnt only by dying, do you wish to stay alive and get the same knowledge by cheating? No way would that be possible."

Kailas Mukherjee often entertained me in my childhood by reciting a long rhyme at breakneck speed. I was the main hero of the poem and there was an undoubted promise of meeting my heroine, brightly described in the stanzas. Here was the most fascinating girl in the world poised gracefully, waiting to be, quite inevitably, mine. My mind was very excited at the prospect. The list of valuable ornaments decorating her whole being and a description of the unforgettable ceremony at the meeting, would have stirred the feelings of even a discerning adult. In order to capture a child's rapt attention and to thrill his mind with all sorts of fantastic and sublime images of happiness was only possible by the unending stream of sounds, swiftly uttered to a swaying rhythm. These are two instances that I still remember of appreciating the sweetness of literature as a child; and I can also remember the rhyme, *'Bristi pore tapur tupur, nade elo baan* – raindrops fall pitter-patter, the brook swells in flood'. This rhyme was like the *Meghdoot* epic of my childhood.

The next event that comes to mind is the starting of school. One day, I saw my elder brother and my nephew Satya who was also older than me, go to school, but I was not considered eligible to go with them. There was no other means of protesting and letting everyone know that I too had the ability, other than by crying loudly. At that time, I had never ridden a car or even stepped outside our home and so, when Satya brightened the description of his journey to school with the most superfluous epithets, my mind could no longer be restrained at home. Our tutor tried to break my spell by the force of a resounding slap and gave me a message with a deep meaning, "Now you are crying to go to school, but just remember, you will have to shed many more tears to stop going." I cannot recollect the tutor's name or his physical features, but his message and the slap on my face are clear in my mind. Such significant and unfailing prediction has never entered my ears in my whole life.

By the force of my loud weeping, I managed to get admitted to The Oriental Seminary ahead of my time. I do not remember at all what lessons I learnt there, but I do remember one method of meting out punishment. If anyone failed to recite his lesson, he was made to stand upright on the bench and the collected slate boards from all the students of the class were loaded on his two extended arms. Whether the gain in physical endurance transferred in any way to the mind, is a subject for debate among behavioural scientists.

In this manner, my education commenced at a very early age. My exposure to literary works started with the books popular among the servants of the house. Primary among them were the Bengali translation of Chanakya's *Slokas* and Krittibas' version of the *Ramayana*. There is one incident about reading the *Ramayana* that stands out in my memory.

It was a cloudy day; I was playing on the veranda in the exterior part of the house. For some reason, Satya wanted to scare me and so he called out loudly, "Policeman, policeman . . . !" I possessed some idea about the duties of policemen. I knew that once a person was handed over to the police, just as a crocodile impaled its victim in its serrated teeth – it was the policeman's moral responsibility to grasp the unfortunate prisoner and disappear into the unseen depths of the police station, just as the crocodile dragged its victim out of sight into the murky water. Unable to figure out how a young boy who has committed no crime could escape from such cruel punishment, I dashed into the secluded portion of the house; a blind fear of being pursued caused my spine to stiffen. I informed my mother about the imminent danger; she did not express any special anxiety. But I did not feel safe to go outside. Grandma, in reality a distant aunt of my mother, used to read the Krittibas *Ramayana* and I picked up her marble paper covered, dog-eared book and sat down on the floor at the entrance to my mother's room with the book on my lap and began reading. In front of me there was a balcony facing the inner courtyard that was lit by the fading daylight of a cloudy late afternoon. Seeing tears streaming down my face caused by the reading of some sorrowful episode in the *Ramayana*, grandma forcibly removed the book from my hands.

Home and Outdoors

IN OUR CHILDHOOD, there was almost no means of amusement. In general, the lifestyle of those days was much simpler than that of today. The resources for display of respectability available to a gentleman then were so few, that today's age would want to disown relationship with him. This being the general characteristic of that period, in our household in addition, the annoying practice of excessive attention towards children was non-existent. In reality, showing affection is for the pleasure of the guardian, for children there is no greater evil.

We were under the rule of the servants of the house. To make their own task simpler, they severely limited our movements. However tough the restrictions are, neglect bestows great independence and in that independence, our minds were free. Our hearts were not imprisoned by feeding, clothing, adorning or embellishing.

There was no finesse in our dining. Our clothes were so simple and few that if a list were to be shown to today's children, there is a risk of loss of respect in their eyes. I never put on a pair of socks before the age of ten. In winter, one simple shirt over another was always enough. We never blamed anyone for our lack of attire. However, when our house-tailor Neyamat Khalifa felt it unnecessary to provide pockets on our shirts, we were unhappy because there is hardly a child born even to the poorest family, who does not have valuable or otherwise possessions to keep in his pocket; by God's grace, between rich and poor households, there is little difference in the concept of what children consider to be their treasure. We each owned a pair of sandals, but these were never under our feet. We used to kick the sandals in front as we walked; the activity was more pushing the footwear rather than moving our feet, thereby defeating the very purpose for which shoes were created.

The activities, dresses, dining and drinking, comfort and pleasures, conversations and discussions of the elder folk were carried out at a distance from us. We could sense what was going on, but it was always beyond our reach. Children today do not take their elders seriously; nothing is forbidden to them and they get whatever they want without asking. We never got anything so easily. Many simple objects were so difficult to come by; we consoled ourselves with the hope that we would be able to possess these as grownups, in the distant future. Because of this attitude, we used to wring the nectar to the fullest from whatever little came our way, wasting neither the rind nor the pit in the process. Nowadays in most well-to-do families, since children get everything so easily, they tend to throw most objects away after half a bite – in their world most things are wasted by misuse.

We spent most of our day in the servants' quarters located on the second floor of the outer portion of the building.

We had a servant named Shyam. He was a dark and well-built youth, with long hair; his home was in the district of Khulna. He made me sit at a fixed spot and drew a boundary line all around with a stick of chalk. He would raise his palm and threaten me with dire consequences if I stepped outside the line. I was not sure whether the danger would come from the devil or from divine sources and this made me very anxious. From my reading of the *Ramayana*, I was well versed with the disaster that befell Sita when she crossed the boundary line around her, and so I could not cast away the threat in utter disbelief.

Just below the window there was a pond with a paved *ghat* or steps descending into the water. Beside the boundary wall near its eastern edge, there stood a gigantic Chinese banyan tree, and to the south there stood a series of coconut palms. Imprisoned in the zone enclosed by the boundary line, I opened the blinds of the window and spent the whole day looking out at the pond as though it were a book of pictures. From early morning, I observed our neighbours coming to bathe, one by one. I even knew who would come when. I was familiar with the characteristics of each person's bathing techniques. A few plugged both their ears with their fingers and hastily executed a few dives before departing; some others did not dive into the water, but wet their *gamcha* towel and repeatedly wrung the water on their heads; some waved their palms about in the water a couple of times to clear the dirty surface, and then suddenly dived in; some jumped in noisily from the upper steps and surrendered to the water; some descended the steps into the water chanting hymns; some were busy, quickly completing the ablutions and hurrying away; yet some others were not in the least busy – these persons would bathe leisurely, chant the holy names, wipe their bodies dry, change their clothes, shake the folds of their dhotis two or three times, pluck some flowers, and very slowly, taking all the time in the world, dispersing the comfort gained from a refreshing bath to the breeze, in a swaying gait commence their journey home. In this fashion, noon would pass and it would be one' o clock. Gradually, the steps going down to the pond would empty of bathers and fall silent. Only the swans and the ducks dove into the water for the whole day searching for tiny snails to eat and preened the feathers on their wings with their beaks.

As the pool grew lonely, the space beneath the banyan tree captured my entire imagination. Prop roots surrounding the main trunk created an intricate zone of darkness beneath the tree. That magical place in an obscure corner of the world, as though by a mistake of some sort, seemed to be beyond all earthly rules. By chance, an impossible and imaginary world, that had escaped the eyes of the Creator, existed there. I would find it impossible to recount clearly the people I saw there in my mind's eye. One day I had addressed the banyan tree thus –

> Night and day you stand upright, hair dreadlocked
> – never free,
> Do you ever recollect that little boy who watched you,
> O ancient banyan tree?

But alas, where is that banyan tree today? The pool, that was the mirror of the presiding deity of the surrounding trees, is also gone; among the bathers, many have followed the footsteps of the departed banyan tree. And that little boy has grown up, spread all sorts of prop roots around him for support as he keeps track of the extremely complex play of light and shadow in the memorable days of his life.

We were forbidden to venture out of the house; even inside, we did not have free access everywhere. Perhaps, that is why I observed the world of nature around me from the shadows. The outdoor was an expansive substance that was beyond my reach and yet, its beauty, sound and smell – through cracks and crannies in doors and windows, from here and from there – reached out and touched me in surprising ways. Through gaps in my prison wall, it tried, many times, to play with me with its myriad gestures. It was free while I was not – there was no way for us to come together, and thus the desire to unite was very strong. Today that dividing line of chalk has vanished, but boundaries still remain. Far is still further on, the outdoor is still outside. The poem, I composed after growing up, comes to my mind:

The caged bird sat in its golden cage,
The wild bird was in the woods, hard to find.
Once by chance, there was a meeting between the two,
Who knows what was in the Lord's mind.
The wild bird says, 'O caged bird, come
Let's fly to the woods together'.
The caged bird says, 'O wild bird, come
Let's live in the privacy of the cage forever'.
The wild bird says, 'No,
I'll never give in to chain'.
The caged bird says, 'Alas!
How will I reach the woods and escape this pain?'

The parapet on the roof terrace of the inner portion of our house was higher than I was. When I grew up a bit and the power exercised by the servants had cooled down somewhat; when there was an arrival of a new bride in the family and I was receiving encouragement to be her companion during her leisure; during that period, on some days, I came up to that terrace in the afternoon. Everyone at home had had their lunch; there was a lull in household activities; everybody in the inner chambers was preoccupied with his siesta; the saris washed after bathing were hung out to dry from the parapet railing; in the corner of the courtyard, the remnants of the afternoon's rice that had been thrown out, attracted a conference of crows. In that lonely leisure time, through gaps in the parapet wall, exchanges between the caged bird and the wild bird took place beak to beak. I used to stand and stare – the series of coconut palms demarking the boundary of our inner garden caught my eyes; through a gap between the trees, a pond in the locality of Singir Bagan could be glimpsed; and beside this pond, there was the cow-shed of the milk-woman who supplied us with milk; further away, amidst green treetops, the Calcutta skyline consisting of roofs of various shapes and sizes reflected the brightness of the afternoon sun and disappeared into the yellow tinged, blue horizon. On the roofs of some of the distant houses, raised attics reared up; it seemed as though, with silently raised hands and extended forefingers, they were trying to wink and attract my attention to some inner mysteries. Just as from outside the palace, a beggar imagines immeasurable treasure of precious gemstones stashed away in locked vaults, so also I imagined that the distant and unknown houses were filled with independence, fun and games that I lacked, to an extent that I cannot describe. Overhead, the sky was a vault of searing brilliance and from its farthest reaches a thin sharp call of an eagle, and in the lane adjacent to Singir Bagan, in front of the houses silently asleep in the heat of midday, an itinerant peddler's plaintive cry, "Bangles, want bangles? Toys, want toys?" – commingled in my ears and filled my entire being with sadness.

My father travelled often and was rarely at home. His chambers on the third floor used to be locked up. I would turn the blinds on the door just enough to reach inside, unlock the deadbolt and enter; in this room there was a sofa on the south end – I lay on this couch and spent quiet afternoons. At the first place it was a room locked away for a long time, entry was barred for all and thus, in that room, there was a definite air of mystery. Besides, there was dazzling sunshine which reflected off the open terrace in front that was bereft of humans which also saddened my mind. On top of it all, there was another attraction. In that period, municipal water supply had just commenced in the city. Since it was a brand new service, its spread was not yet being curtailed from Bengali localities. Its spread was equal both in the north and in the south of the city. Even in the *satyajuga*, or early days of domestic water supply in Kolkata, water flowed through the pipe in my father's third floor bathroom. There, I used to take untimely showers, lingering to my heart's content. I did not really need to bathe; I did it just to give free rein to my desire. On the one hand there was freedom, on the other there was a fear of being caught; both sensations combined to make the piped stream of the Company's water rain arrows of thrill on my mind.

Since I did not have much physical interaction with the world outside, it was perhaps easier for me to enjoy it even more. If the ways and means are many, the mind becomes lazy, a person then becomes wholly dependent on the physical presence of external objects for his happiness; he forgets that in the feast of happiness, rather than what is outside, it is the inner celebration that is more important. This is the very first lesson of childhood for all humans. Then, his means are few and insignificant, but for seeking happiness he does not need much else. The unfortunate child, who gets an unlimited supply of toys, loses the charm of his playtime.

To call the open space in our compound a garden would be an overstatement. A grapefruit tree, an Indian jujube tree, a hog plum tree and a line of coconut palm provided the only justification. At the centre, there was a paved terrace. Along its crack lines, grasses and all sorts of weeds planted their flags of unauthorised occupation. Few hardy flowering plants that do not die due to lack of care, continued to follow their line of duty fearlessly with all their might, without bothering to complain against the gardener. In a corner of the north side, there was a shelter that housed a paddy husker where the residents of the inner mansion assembled sometimes purely to satisfy the needs of the family. Realising that village life cannot exist in a city like Kolkata, one day, that shelter with the paddy husker quietly hid its face and disappeared. That Adam's Garden of Eden was much more decorated than our garden is something I do not believe. This is because the Garden of Eden was without any cover – Adam made no arrangements to conceal himself. After eating the forbidden fruit from the tree of knowledge, until man is able to completely digest the fruit, his need to dress and decorate himself is ever increasing. The garden in our compound was my Garden of Eden – it was enough for me. I remember very well that on early mornings in autumn, as soon as I opened my eyes, I came out to this garden. The fragrance of grass and leaves damp with night dew rushed to fill my senses, just as with delicate new sun rays breaking between the top of the east boundary wall and the gently trembling fronds of the coconut trees, day-break announced itself.

There was another piece of vacant land on the north side of our house, which to this day we know as *golabari*, or the granary. The name is proof of the fact, that in older times a granary was built there to store excess crops after a harvest – then city and village, like very young brother and sister, appeared to look alike; now it is difficult to find any similarity at all, between the elder sister and her brother.

On a holiday, if I got a chance, I used to present myself at the *golabari*. It would not be right to say that I went there to play. More than any game, this place by itself, attracted me. It is difficult to pinpoint a reason. It was a lonely, abandoned, burnt-out corner of the compound – perhaps because of that the place held a mystery for me. It was not a living area for us, not a room we used; it had no function; it was way outside the main residence with no signs of everyday use and it was an ugly unnecessary fallow land on which no one had bothered even to plant flowers; that is why on that barren piece of land, a boy's mind had no bar to boundless imagination. If ever I could escape my protectors through the slightest chink in their armours and come away here, it seemed like a holiday to me.

There was another place in our house, which to this day, I have been unable to locate. My playmate, a girl of my age, used to call it the king's palace. Sometimes I heard her say, "I went there today." But I never had an opportunity of accompanying her. It appeared to be an amazing place where the games were wonderful and the toys were marvellous. It seemed to be somewhere very close; a place either on the main floor or on the first; but, it never happened that we could reach that place. Time and again I asked the girl, "Is the king's palace inside our building, or is it outside?" Every time she replied, "No, it is inside here." Astounded, I used to sit and think that I had seen each and every room in this building, now where could this palace be? I never asked who the king was; where his kingdom lay, is undiscovered to this day; the only indication available is that the king's palace was within our house.

Looking back at my childhood there is one thing I remember most: that life and the world around, was full of mystery. That, everywhere, there existed something unimaginable and there was no way of knowing when it would reveal itself – I used to battle with this dilemma every day. Nature would extend a clenched fist and smilingly ask, "Let's see you tell me what's inside." What really was not possible, I could not say for certain.

I remember very well that I had planted a seed of custard-apple in a pot located in the corner of our veranda. Just thinking about the possibility that the seed may grow into a tree one day, tremendous amazement and curiosity would take birth in my mind. Custard-apple seeds grow into seedlings even today, but the same sense of wonder no longer germinates in my mind. It is not the fault of the custard-apple seeds, the fault lies with the mind. We stole stones from Guna-dada's rock garden and busied ourselves in making a mock hill in the corner of our study – we planted flowering plants and in the name of caring, we pestered them to such an extent that they remained silent simply because they were merely plants; and, they did not hesitate to die. I cannot describe enough, the pleasure and amazement that the hill gave us. Deep in our hearts, we felt convinced that our creation would be a fabulous object to the elders as well; when we set out to test our conviction, on that very day, our hill, in the corner of the study complete with its flora, disappeared somewhere. That the corner of the study was not a suitable location for founding a hill – getting this lesson in such a sudden and harsh fashion made us feel very sorry for ourselves. Reminded of the fact that there was such a wide gap between our concept of pleasure and what the elders wished, the task of supporting the foundation of the family shifted the weight of its burden onto our minds.

It keeps coming to my mind that in those days, the flavour of this object called Earth was so very intense. Whether it was the soil, or water, or vegetation, or sky, everything used to speak to me – they never let my mind be disinterested even for a moment. That I was able to see only the upper levels of Earth, and never what lay below, troubled my mind to an extent I cannot describe. I made countless plans of how the brown coloured upper cover of Earth could be peeled away. I used to think that if it were possible to drive one length of bamboo after another, somehow we might be able to touch the deepest reaches of Earth. On the occasion of the festival in the month of *Magh*, wooden pillars were erected all around our courtyard to hang chandeliers from. The earthworks commenced from the first of the month. All over the world, the starting of the preparations for a festival is an activity of great interest to children. But the cutting of the earth held a special attraction for me. Even though, I watched the digging every year – observed the hole getting bigger little by little until the digger disappeared from sight in its depths, I never perceived anything that would make the journey of a prince or any noble man's son to the netherworld successful – even then each and every time, I felt the lid of a mystery chest open. I wished that the men would dig a little more; but year after year, that extra digging was never accomplished. The curtain was always tugged a little bit aside, but never moved completely. I wondered, that if the grownups wished, they could get anything done, then why were they stuck in the shallows – if we children could have our way, then news from the deepest recesses of Earth wouldn't lie buried listlessly in the soil. Besides, behind the blueness of the sky was hidden all its mystery – this thought too disturbed my mind. The day when our teacher mentioned, perhaps in the course of a lesson, that the blue heaven above was not a restriction at all, it filled my mind with tremendous awe. He said, "If you keep placing a ladder on a ladder and continue moving upwards, even then, your head will not strike against anything." I thought he was being an undue miser with ladders. I kept intoning, "More ladders, more ladders, more ladders . . . ", until it dawned on me that increasing the ladder count was of no use; and then, I sat down in utter astonishment and thought, that only teachers could possibly have such a surprising piece of information, and nobody else.

The Servant-rule Scriptures

IN MEDIEVAL INDIAN history, the period under the rule of the slave dynasty was not a particularly happy one. In the history of my life too, whenever I look back at the period of servant-rule, I cannot perceive any charm or happiness. The slave-kings changed from one to the next frequently, but there never was any difference in our fortunes with respect to prohibition and punishment. We never had the opportunity to discuss right and wrong – we received whatever blows that rained on our backs, knowing that this was the way of the world – the big and powerful meted out punishment and the small and weak always accepted it. The contrary fact, that here it was the person of lower standing who administered the beating and it was the person of higher standing who accepted it, took a lot of time for me to realise.

What is naughty and what is well-behaved, the bird-hunter never gets to see that from the bird's eyes, but always from his own. That is why the hunter curses the alert bird, which cries out aloud before a shot is fired and cautions its flock. When we cried after being beaten, the servants did not consider it to be good manners. They considered it to be an act of sedition against them. I remember very well that attempts were made to completely suppress that sedition by imprisoning us inside large water jars and thereby choking out our wailing. No one will disown the argument that wailing is not only undesirable to the aggressors but also inconvenient.

Now, I sometimes wonder, why we received such cruel treatment from the hands of our servants. I cannot say that physically we were unsuitable for love and affection. The actual reason is that, our entire burden fell on the servants. Complete burden is very difficult to bear. It is unbearable even to the closely related. If a young child is allowed to be a young child – if he can play, run and exhaust his curiosity, only then is he going to be easily managed. But if you think that you will not let him go out, obstruct his playing, calm him down and make him sit still, then an extremely unbearable problem is bound to be created.

That is to say, the burden that a child, through his childlike behaviour, is very well capable of supporting on his own, now falls on the supervisor. It is akin to the situation where a horse is not allowed to trot on the ground, but is carried on the back of his keeper. The poor fellow who shoulders the load cannot keep his temper. He goes on slaving for the sake of an allowance, but exacts revenge on the poor horse at every step.

The memories of many of these disciplinarians of our childhood are merely in the form of slaps and blows – I do not remember anything more than that. Only the memory of one person comes to my mind very clearly.

His name was Iswar. Earlier he used to be a village priest. Though extremely obsessive about ritual purity and conducting himself by the scriptures, he was a learned and serious-natured man. There was a great paucity of earth and water on this planet that could support the preservation of his virtuousness. Consequently, he seemed to constantly battle the corpse-like uncleanliness of this Earth. With lightning speed he would dip his *ghati*, or mug in the pond and collect water from three- to four-feet depth. During his bath, for a long time, he would use his two hands to wave away the water at the upper level and then suddenly dive in with great speed; as if, by somehow distracting the pond, his primary intention was to sneak in and wet his head. While walking, his left arm used to travel in such a manner – a little crookedly independent of his body – that, it became very obvious that his right arm did not have faith in even the cleanliness of the clothes that covered him. In water, land, sky and humanity, pollution lurked in every pore and opening, and it was his severely austere vow to steer clear of all these. It was unbearable to him, if the world at large came even a bit close to his body. His personality was dominated by his serious demeanour. Head tilted slightly towards one side, he spoke slowly, chewing every word. Our guardians often laughed at his use of the refined written language in speech. There was a saying about him at home that he used to pronounce the locality called Baranagar as Barahanagar, or the City of Pigs. This may be just hearsay, but I know that instead of 'someone is waiting in the drawing room', he had announced, 'someone is awaiting your presence in the drawing room'. Instances of his use of the refined written language while speaking were stored in the family humour collection for many days. Surely, it is no longer funny to hear 'someone is awaiting your presence' from the lips of a servant of a respectable household. From this, it is clear that the language of contemporary Bengali literature is moving down to the coarse spoken form, whereas the spoken language is moving up towards the more refined written form; the heaven and earth disparity that once existed between the two is gradually dissipating.

This erstwhile priest devised a means of keeping us all quietly together in the evenings. After dark, we were made to sit surrounding an array of burning oil lamps, while he read aloud from the *Ramayana* or the *Mahabharata*. From among the other servants, a few came to listen. The faint light threw massive shadows that reached up to the roof beams; geckos on the walls hunted insects; small bats flew in circles along the upper reaches of the veranda, rotating like fervent dervishes; while we sat with slack jaws, listening to Iswar's narration. The day the battle scene was being narrated where the youth of the epic were busy smiting their fathers and uncles to dust, I remember to this moment, how on that evening, our assembly in the weak lamp-light became united in spellbound silence. It was late and our time to stay up was running out, but the conclusion was still far. At this critical juncture, our father's personal servant, Kishori Chatterjee, came in and completed the rest of the episode at a fast pace, reading a different version of the epic from Dasuray's *Panchali;* the gentle sounds of the simple rhymes in the Krittibas version were completely obliterated – the brightness and thunder of the alliteration in the *Panchali* left us dumbfounded.

On some days during the reading of the epics, when arguments over the scriptures broke out in the audience, Iswar used his deep knowledge to settle the issues. Even though his status in the servant's society was lower than many others for his serving only children, still, like the great grandfather *Bhisma* of the *Kaurava* clan in the epic *Mahabharata,* seated as he was lower than his juniors, he was able to maintain his pride as a guru undisturbed.

This very venerable protector of ours had a weakness that I am being forced to reveal for the sake of historical veracity. He was addicted to opium. For this reason, he needed a particularly nutritious diet. That is why, when he brought our quota of milk in front of us, his attraction towards the milk proved far greater than disinterest. If we expressed our customary unwillingness to drink milk – not even for the sake of fulfilling his duty towards upkeep of our good health – he never requested twice or forced us in any way.

Iswar also had a strong inclination to curtail our breakfast. We would sit down to eat. *Luchi*, or deep fried flat bread, used to be piled high in a large wooden bowl in front of us. He usually picked a few from the top of the pile, and preserving his ritual purity by avoiding touching anything else, he flung these on to our plates from a height. Like a boon that is forcibly collected by the power of penance despite the unwillingness of the Gods, the few pieces of *luchi* rained on our plates; in the process, the ritually polluted left hand of the server never once appeared. After that, Iswar asked whether we needed any more. I knew which answer he would count as the most truthful. I did not feel like asking for a second serving by denying him his share. He got money to buy us things for our breakfast from the market. He asked us every day what we wished to eat. I knew that if I requested inexpensive foodstuff, he would be pleased. Sometimes I asked for puffed rice with suitable accompaniments, or some other time it was soaked gram and fried peanuts or something equally unhealthy. I noticed that the fervour he displayed in the ritual observance of scriptural prescriptions was lacking in matters related to our health and diet.

Normal School

WHEN I WAS studying at the Oriental Seminary, I found a way out to overcome the indignity of merely being a student. In a special corner of our veranda, I too set up a classroom. The handrail posts were my students. A cane in hand, I sat in front of them on a stool, and practiced teaching. Among the handrail posts, it was pre-decided who was a good boy and who was not. Not only that, I clearly perceived the difference in the facial structures of the good and the naughty, the clever and the foolish, hand rail posts. The naughty ones were in such a pitiable state from the lashings of my cane, that if they possessed lives, they would have gladly given that up for the sake of a little peace. The more they grew distorted from my onslaught, the stronger my fury was directed at them; I could not think up any other means of delivering adequate punishment to the erring students. On my poor class of speechless students, I exercised a terrifying teaching ordeal for which there is no witness alive to this day. In place of the wooden handrail students from my days, iron handrails have taken admission – from among our next generation, no one has accepted the responsibility to teach the new students as yet, and even if someone did, yesterday's teaching methods would not yield any results today. I have observed well that children are very late in learning the lessons conferred on them by their teachers, but they rarely have any difficulty in picking up the teacher's attitude. All aspects of injustice, impatience, rage and misbalanced outlook inherent in the process of granting education, I was able to internalise more easily than the subjects worth learning. The only happy aspect is that, other than on objects as speechless and unmoving as wooden handrails, I did not get an opportunity to practice my barbarous methods at that helplessly early age. Even though there were enough differences between the handrail class and the student class, between me and the narrow-minded teachers, there was hardly any difference in mental make-up.

I believe I did not study at the Oriental Seminary for long. After that I got admitted to Normal School. I was still at a very tender age. There is one thing I remember – each morning before the school started, all boys would assemble in the gallery and recite some sort of poetry set to tune like a song. It must have been an attempt to arrange some amount of entertainment to accompany the boys' education. But the words of the songs were in English, and so was the tune – I did not understand any of the hymns we chanted and nor could I appreciate the occasion. To participate in a meaningless and boring affair on a daily basis was not in the least pleasurable to us. However, the school authorities had adopted the event from contemporary theatre and they were convinced that, in the process, they were spreading happiness among the students; but they felt it completely unnecessary to observe the boys' reactions every day and judge the outcome. It was as though they expected that by following the theatrical practice, it was the duty of the boys to feel entertained; and not to do so, was their crime. That is why they had selected a play from an English book and having taken an entire song out of that for us to sing, they felt contented. From our lips, the English that emerged was transformed into another language, the identification of which can doubtlessly be the topic of valuable discussion among language specialists. There is only one line I can remember:

Kaloki puloki shingal mellaling mellaling mellaling.

After much contemplation, I have been successful in deciphering most of the lyrics – but from what word the sound *'kaloki'* could have been derived beats me to this day. The rest perhaps, can be read as:

. . . full of glee, singing merrily, merrily, merrily.

Subsequent memories of Normal School cross the foggy state into a clearer form, but no part of it is in any way sweeter. If only I could have interacted with my co-students then, perhaps my disappointment in the education process would have been less unbearable. But that did not happen in any way. The company of most students was so unclean and insulting, that I would sit with a servant beside a window facing the road on the second floor, just to be alone during the closing hour. I used to count in my mind – one year, two years, three years . . . – wondering how many more years I would have to spend in this manner. Among the teachers, I remember one person who used such uncouth language, that out of sheer lack of respect towards him, I refused to answer any of his questions. For an entire year, I sat in silence at the back of the class, behind all students. As the class went on, it gave me some respite to try and resolve many difficult problems facing the world. There is one issue I remember well. How to defeat the enemy in a battle, while being unarmed oneself was a subject of deep contemplation for me. Seated in that classroom, surrounded by the humming sound of a lesson in progress, I can still remember deliberating that question in my mind. I thought that if dogs, tigers and other such ferocious animals could be brought under control and arranged in the first few rows of the battlefield, then the very start of the war would easily become more interesting; thereafter, if one's own army's strength was exercised, victory over the enemy could not be particularly impossible. Whenever I imagined this easy method of preparing for war, I pictured a certain victory for our side in the battlefield. When I did not have much to do, I devised surprisingly easy methods to do work. Now when I am actually working, I can see, that what is tough, stays tough; what is impossible, stays impossible; exceptions notwithstanding, trying to make things easier actually complicates the problem many fold.

In this manner, when a year passed in that class. We faced the paper set by Madusudhan Bachaspati as we took our annual examination of the Bengali language. I scored higher marks than anyone else in the class. Our teacher informed the school authorities that he, as an examiner, suspected my performance. A second examination was held for me. On this occasion, the superintendent himself sat on a stool beside the examiner. Luckily, even at that instance, I secured a high position.

The Beginnings of Poetry

I WAS NO MORE than seven or eight years old at that time. One of my nephews Srijukta Jyotiprakash, was elder to me by more than a few years. He had just entered the world of English literature, and, with great enthusiasm, he used to recite Hamlet's introductory speech. Why he suddenly developed a passion to make a child like me write poetry, I cannot say for certain. He called me into his room one afternoon and declared, "You have to write poetry." Then he explained the methods of connecting fourteen syllables in the *payar* rhyme form, popular in those days.

So far, I had only seen poetry printed in books. Nothing was crossed out, the thought process behind the composition was not revealed and there never were any signs of mortal fear. That writing such poems could even be attempted I did not have the courage to imagine. One day a thief was captured at home. Very fearful and yet extremely curious, I went to see him. I saw that he was just like any ordinary man. At this juncture when the watchman began raining blows on him, I felt hurt inside. My condition regarding poetry turned out to be the same. When the few words I was able to connect together on my own developed into a rhyme, I no longer had any more interest in composing poems. Now I can see that poor poetry cannot withstand blows either. Sometimes I feel pity and yet, my hands itch and it is impossible to resist a few blows. So many blows never landed, even on the thief's back.

When I lost my fear, there was no keeping me in check. With the assistance of one of our employees, I got hold of a notebook made out of blue paper. I drew a few uneven lines on a page and in large childish letters I started writing poetry.

Just as a young deer, starting to grow new antlers, jumps around butting here and there, with my newly acquired knowledge of poetry, I too began a similar sort of pestering. Especially it was dada or my elder brother, who out of pride at my compositions, went about collecting audiences, and in his enthusiasm, made everyone's life in the family quite unbearable. I remember one day, dada and I were just preparing to display our poetic skill in front of the employees of our estate, when the then editor of 'The National Paper', Srijukta Nabagopal Mitra just entered our house. Immediately dada captured him and said, "Nabagopal-babu, Rabi has written a poem, so why don't we listen to it?" There was no delay in presenting my poem. My collection of poetry was still not very heavy. The poet's works were mobile, easily accommodated in the pocket of the poet's shirt. I alone, was the sole writer, type-setter and publisher rolled into one. Only as far as advertising was required, dada was my co-worker. I had composed a poem on the lotus flower, which, standing at the main entranceway, I recited in a loud excited voice for Nabagopal-babu. He laughed and remarked, "Well composed, but what does the word *dwiref* mean?"

Dwiref and *bhramor* are synonyms for the bee in Bengali, both words having three syllables. I could have easily used the more commonplace *bhramor* without affecting the rhyme in any way. I do not recollect from where I managed to get the more difficult word. In the whole poem, I placed a lot of hope on that one word. Surely, I was able to impress the assembly of our employees by the use of that word. But it did not affect Nabagopal-babu in the least. Not only that, he even laughed. I firmly believed then, that Nabagopal-babu did not appreciate poetry. I never read him another poem. Since then I have grown much older, but I do not think that there has been much change in my method of judging the true appreciator from one who is not. In any case, Nabagopal-babu laughed all right, but the word *dwiref*, like a bee drunk with honey, remained undisturbed in its place.

Preparations for Other Learning

IN THOSE DAYS, a teacher from Normal School, Srijukta Nilkamal Ghosal Mahasay, used to teach us at home. His body was weak and dried out and his voice was thin and sharp. He seemed like a slim cane born in a human form. It was his duty to teach us from six to nine-thirty every morning. We learnt from him a number of things, starting from rapid reading, elementary physics and life science to Michael's *Meghnadbadh* epic poem. Sej-dada, or my third elder brother, was very keen in our acquisition of knowledge in diverse fields. We learnt much more at home than we did at school. We had to wake up in the darkness of early morning, and clad in our loin cloths, grapple with a blind wrestler. After that, we put on our clothes on our muddied bodies and then we had to learn physical science, *Meghnathbadh*, geometry, arithmetic, history and geography. As soon as we returned from school, the teachers for drawing and for gymnastics would get busy with us. Aghar-babu came in the evening to teach us English. In this way, our day ended only after nine o'clock in the evening.

Sunday mornings, we had to take singing lessons from Bishnu. Besides that, Satinath Dutta Mahasay used to come by regularly to teach us practical natural sciences, using various apparatuses. These lessons held special interest for me. In a pot placed over fire, heated water from below grows less dense and moves up while the denser and colder water from the top moves down, and that is why water boils – when he added sawdust into a glass vessel of water and put it on a stove and demonstrated the phenomenon before our eyes, I still remember to this day, how amazed I had been. Water in milk is an independent medium which evaporates as steam when milk is heated, leaving milk denser – the day I understood this process clearly, I was very pleased. The Sunday morning on which he failed to come did not feel like a Sunday to me at all.

Apart from this, at some time, we started learning human anatomy from a student of the Campbell Medical School. A human skeleton, held together by wire was acquired and hung on the wall of our study.

In the middle of all this, at one time, Heramba Tarkaratna Mahasay started teaching us *slokas* on Lord Krishna as well as grammar in Sanskrit, to be learnt by heart. Between the names of bones in Latin and the sutras by Bopdeb, I cannot tell for certain which was victorious. Perhaps to me, the bones were easier.

When our education in Bengali had progressed quite far, we started our lessons in English. Our tutor, Aghar-babu used to study in the medical college. He came to teach us in the evenings. I have read that creating fire from wood was perhaps the greatest discovery of mankind. I do not deny that. However, it comes to my mind that in the evenings, birds cannot light lamps and this is a great blessing for the chicks. They learn their language during the day and joyfully, you might have noticed. Of course, it is worth remembering that it is not English that they learn.

This gentleman medical student was of such sound health that despite wishes from the depths of the minds of his three students, he never had to take a day off. There was only one instance, where, after a faceoff between the White students and their Bengali counterparts, the enemy had flung a stool at him and fractured his skull. No doubt it was a serious matter, but we were unable to consider his fractured forehead as our bad luck, and his recovery had seemed unnecessarily quick.

It was evening; there was a heavy downpour; the road was flooded to a knee's depth. Our pond was filled to the brim. The *bel* fruit trees raised their tousled heads above the water; the delight of a rainy evening thrilled my mind like the *kadamba* flower in mythology. A few minutes had passed beyond the usual arrival time of our tutor. However, nothing could be concluded as yet. I sat on a stool in the veranda facing the street in front of the house and stared longingly towards the point where the street turned away from sight. I was reduced to the anxious state of a leaf quivering under falling drops as in a line from the poet Jaydeva. Suddenly my heart jumped violently. The black umbrella, unvanquished even in a divine wrought calamity, was visible at a distance. Could it be somebody else? No, it just couldn't. It might be possible to get another poet of similar calibre as Bhababhuti on this earth, but on that rainy evening, it was impossible for anyone similar to our tutor to make an appearance.

When I look back, I can see that Aghar-babu was not particularly a strict tutor-type of person. He never used his physical strength to control us. His reprimands hardly contained loud outbursts. However good a person he might have been, he taught us in the evening, and his subject was English. After all the sorrows of a long day, in the dim light of a lantern, even if an angel had been given the responsibility of teaching English to Bengali boys, there's no doubt in my mind that he would have seemed like a messenger from hell. I can remember well, that one day, Aghar-babu took it upon himself to prove to us that English is not a dull language; as an example of its wit and humour – I do not remember whether it was prose or poetry – he recited a piece in English with a mesmerised expression. To us it felt very strange. We cracked up in laughter to such an extent that he had to break off, realising that the case would not be an easy one – to get a decree of victory, he would have to do battle for the next ten to fifteen years.

Sometimes, our *mastermosai* tried to inject the freshness of the south wind from outside the dreary desert realm of printed books. All of a sudden one day, he took out a mysterious paper wrapped object from his pocket and declared, "Today, I am going to show all of you a wondrous creation of God." He un-wrapped the package to display a human larynx and began to explain its function. I remember well the shock I experienced. I thought that the whole human being spoke; I had no idea that the act of speaking could be broken down to its components in this manner. A particular mechanism might be an object of wonder, but it could never surpass the whole being. Of course, I had not been able to reason then, but my mind felt a bit sorrowful; I was unable to join in *mastermosai*'s enthusiasm. In the act of dissecting the human body, perhaps *mastermosai* had forgotten that the mystery of human speech arose from deep within and not merely in the voice-box; that is why, his explanation of the function of the larynx did not ring true in the boy's mind. After that, one day, he took us to the dissection room of the medical college. A cadaver of an old woman lay on the table; that sight didn't excite me very much; but the sight of a severed human leg on the table startled my entire mind considerably. To see a piece of a human body was so dreadful, so unreasonable, that I was unable to forget the vision of the dark, severed leg on the table for many days.

No sooner than we had completed the first and second parts of the English lesson book by Parry, that a volume of Michael's Course of Reading was thrust into our hands. In the evening, with our bodies exhausted and our minds diverted to the inner parts of the house, the book with its thick black cover and difficult language appeared to be bereft of kindness, for I had not observed any motherly feeling in *Saraswati*, the Goddess of Learning, towards children in those days. There were no illustrations on every page as in the books for children today. At the beginning of every text book, there used to be arrays of words, which, with their syllables separated by hyphens and accent symbols raised as sharp lances, seemed to threaten war. We made little progress banging our heads against the pitiless fortress wall of English language. On top of this, every day, *mastermosai* would cite the example of an exemplary student, just to shame us. This kind of comparison did not generate any liking towards that student; we were ashamed and yet the darkness in the book stayed undiminished. The divine in nature, out of sheer kindness towards living beings, had bestowed sleep inducing capacity in all unintelligible subjects. As soon as we began our lessons, our heads would roll over in sleep. Flinging water in the eyes or being made to run the length of the veranda had no permanent effect. At such times, by some miracle, if while walking on the veranda, bar-dada, our eldest brother, happened to see our piteous sleepy condition, he would stop the lessons. Once this happened, it took just a few moments for our sleep to vanish for good.

Journey to the World Outside

ONCE, DRIVEN BY an outbreak of dengue, some from our extended family were forced to seek shelter in the estates belonging to Chatu-babu at Peniti. We were among them.

This was the first time I truly ventured outside our home. The banks of the Ganges welcomed me into an embrace, as though in recognition of a relationship from a previous life. In front of the servants' quarters there were a handful of guava trees. Seated in the shade of the veranda, I spent my days looking at the Ganges, screened from view by the guava grove. Every morning, the moment I awoke, it seemed that the day was being gifted to me like a newly arrived letter in a gilded envelope. If I opened the envelope, I might be greeted by some wonderful news. Lest

I lose even a bit of the message, I would hurriedly wash my face and then take position on a low stool in the veranda. The daily ebb and flow of the tide on the Ganges; the variety of movements of the different types of boats on the water; the gradual shifting of the shadow of the guava grove from west to east; on the banks near Konnagar, the deluge of gold and red of the setting sun on the darkness of the arrayed woods – all seemed to signify the sorrow for the end of the day. On some mornings, clouds would appear in the sky; the trees on the far shore would darken; the river would be in shadow; in no time, the horizon disappeared in the driving rain and the far shore line seemed to dissolve in tears; the river swelled and the moisture-laden wind wilfully bent the branches of trees on this shore.

Freed from the womb-like confines of ceiling beams and walls, I was born again in the larger world outside. In my attempts to discover everything anew, the cover of familiarity over the world I knew gradually disintegrated. The chunk of unrefined sugar with which I ate previous day's *luchi* in the morning was in no way less sweet than the heavenly nectar of the Lord Indra. The ambrosia is not in the drink, it lies in the ability to appreciate – this is why, it eludes all those who search for it.

Behind the place we sat, there was a pond in a courtyard enclosed by walls, with paved steps leading down to the water – and beside the *ghat*, there stood a *jamrul*, or bell-fruit tree; all around large fruit trees thickly surrounded the pond, their shadows creating a veil to guard her modesty. The veiled beauty of this covered, enclosed, shaded and protected little courtyard garden was in my mind, beyond compare. How different this place was when compared to the lofty openness of the shores of the Ganges. This was like the woman of the house. In her shaded corner, she spread her quilt embroidered with green leaves and tendrils, and in the privacy of midday, gently expressed her innermost thoughts. On such middays, I sat in the shade of the *jamrul* tree and imagined the abode of a *yaksha* beneath the pond, a suspenseful world of untold stashed-away riches.

For many days, I was eager to see a village of Bengal in detail. Imagined homes, domestic shrines, play grounds and rural livelihoods strongly attracted my heart to villages. There was such a village immediately adjacent to our garden on the shores of the Ganges – but it was forbidden to us. We had ventured outdoors, but we were not free. Like pet birds, we used to live in cages; now we perched on a stand, but our feet still remained in shackles.

One day, two of my many guardians, set out for a walk in the neighbourhood. Unable to control my curiosity for the world outside, unnoticed, I set out behind them. Along village by-lanes shaded by deep woods and beside algae-green ponds separated from the road by a rough fence I walked, and in great happiness, continued to paint a picture in my mind of the unfolding surroundings. A man brushing his teeth with a twig, as late in the day as it was then, has stayed in my memory to this day. At that moment, the persons ahead suddenly realised that I was following them. They exclaimed loudly, "Go, go; go back at once." They thought I was not dressed properly to go outside. I had no socks to cover my feet, no jacket or shawl over my shirt – this they considered to be my fault. But I did not possess socks or any other suitable pieces of dress and so, not only did I have to return disappointed on that day, I had no means of correcting my faults and venturing outdoors on another occasion.

Behind me the obstacles remained, but in front, the Ganges absolved me of all bondage. My mind jumped on sail boats without bothering to pay the fare and undertook long voyages to imagined lands which are yet to be discovered.

All these happened over forty years ago. Since then, I have never again set foot on the blossom covered bathing *ghat* of that garden. The trees and the building still exist no doubt, but I know the garden does not; since a garden is not made up of plants and trees, it is built with the pleasure derived from the newly discovered sense of wonder in a child – and can I ever rediscover that sense of wonder again?

I returned home to the Jorasanko mansion. My days went on, passing through the gaping maw of Normal school, as a mere morsel of its daily quota.

Composing Poetry

THE NOTEBOOK WITH blue coloured pages gradually filled up like an insect's nest with irregular letters on crooked lines. It was distorted with the eager forceful lettering of a child. Steadily, it grew tattered and the edges tore into strips, which, like many fingers, contained the writings within its tight fist. The merciful Goddess of Oblivion has sailed away with that blue notebook and there is no fear any longer of its existence on Earth. It has managed to escape the pain of the printing press.

Surely, I was not worried about publicising the fact that I wrote poetry. Though Satkori Dutta Mahasay was not my teacher, he had a special fondness towards me. He had written a volume on life science. I hope no adept humorist will attribute the cause of Satkori Dutta Mahasay's affection towards me to the topic and contents of his book. He took me aside one day and asked, "Do you compose poetry?" I did not try to hide the fact that I did. After this, in order to encourage me, he began to give me a few lines of poetry now and then to take home and complete. I can remember one –

All were troubled by the sun's blazing power,
Rains assured – no further need to cower.

Of the accompanying poem I composed, I can remember a couple of lines. In order to prove that my poetry in those days was far from being difficult to comprehend, I am taking the liberty of recording on print –

Fishes lived in the lake, humiliated every day,
Now, in happiness they swim and play.

Whatever depth there is in the writing, relates to the lake – that is very clear.

Let me present four lines from another composition, hoping that in the world of poetry, the language and expression will be considered as lucid –

Dried mango pulp in milk, ripe banana kneaded in,
With *sandesh* in the mix –
Slurping noises, disturb the silence,
While ants scurry, crying for share of the fix.

Gobinda-babu from our school was a short and stout man. He was the superintendent. Clad in a black coat, he used to be busy with notebooks in his second floor office. We were scared of him. He was the dispenser of punishment in the school. One day, unable to put up with any more torment, I rushed into his chambers. The guilty party consisted of five to six boys bigger than me; there was no witness on my side. My tears were my sole witness. I emerged victorious in that encounter, though the incident made Gobinda-babu look at me with pity.

One day after classes, I received a call to his office. No sooner than I presented myself trembling in front of him, that he asked, "Do you write poetry?" I didn't hesitate a moment to admit that I did. I do not recollect what high moral subject he ordered me to compose a poem with. Such an order, from the lips of someone with as serious a demeanour as Gobinda-babu, was so strangely sweet, that anyone, who has not been taught by him, cannot possibly imagine. When I wrote the poem and showed it to him next day, he took me along with him to the class of students with scholarships and made me stand in front of them. He ordered, "Read it to them." I recited the lines loudly.

There is only one reason that this highly moral poem can be praised – that it got lost early. Its moral effect on the scholarship-students was far from hopeful. At least, no good feeling towards the poet was generated in the audience. Most boys were heard muttering that the poem was definitely not composed by me. One among them declared that he could bring the book from which I had stolen the poem and show it to the class. No one begged him to do so. They wanted to believe – any attempt at proof might have been counterproductive to their cause. After this event, the number of those seeking fame through poetry began to rise. The path they chose was not one of moral redemption.

Nowadays it is not surprising for young boys to write poetry. The vanity of poetry has been completely knocked down.

I remember well that in those days, the one or two women who wrote poems were considered as astonishing creations of God. Now, if I hear of any woman who does not write poetry, it seems so impossible that I find it hard to believe. Poetic skill germinates early these days, even without any encouragement and well before achieving the class of scholarship-students. Thus, the doings of the child that I have narrated here will not surprise any modern day Gobinda-babu.

Srikantha-babu

AROUND THIS TIME, I gained a great listener and I am certain that I will never find another like him. He was such a likeable person that it would be impossible for him to even be the subject of a brief literary criticism. He was as pleasant as a ripened 'Bombay' mango – without a trace of sourness – and his personality was like the flesh of the fruit that had no fibres in it. He had a bald pate and a sweet face that was clean shaven, his gums were toothless and his large eyes glinted with laughter. When he spoke in his habitually deep voice, his entire body grew animated and seemed to join in. He belonged to the earlier generation educated in Persian and was a witty person who did not care very much about English. He always had a hookah on his left side; wherever he sat, on his lap there rested a sitar and his vocal chords forever trilled with song.

Acquainted or otherwise, there was no doubt that by the sheer force of his warm-heartedness he could extend his control over most individuals. I remember very well that he took us to a British photographer's shop to have our picture taken. He struck up a conversation in Hindi and Bengali to develop rapport; and as though to a near relative, he was able to speak so forcefully – "there is no way I can pay so much to have our picture taken, I am but a poor man; no, no *sahib*, it is not possible at all" – that the *sahib* had to acquiesce and take the picture for a lower fee. His most unreasonable request, in a strict British establishment, did not feel the least untoward, since his normal relation with all humans was just as unhindered – he had no hesitation to approach anyone, since there was no reason in his mind for any hesitation.

On some days, he used to take me along with him to the house of a European missionary. There, he would win over his audience like nobody else could, by his singing, by his sitar playing, by his show of affection towards the gentleman's daughters and by his repeated praise for their tiny feet laced in boots. Such behaviour from anyone else would have been considered annoying, but it was definitely not the case as far as Srikantha-babu was concerned – thus everyone would laugh along with him and be happy.

Then again, no miscreant could ever hurt him. Attempted insults never landed on him as insults. A famous singer was once a resident of our home for long time. In a drunken state he used to heap abuse on Srikantha-babu, but the latter accepted the insults without a protest and with a smile on his face. In the end, because of his boorish behaviour towards Srikantha-babu, it was decided that the famed singer should leave our house. At this development, Srikantha-babu tried to defend his tormentor. He said repeatedly, "He hasn't done anything wrong, the fault lies with the alcohol he drinks."

Not only could he not bear to see anyone hurt, he could not tolerate sorrowful tales. In order to pull his leg, when some boy attempted to trouble him by reading aloud a sorrowful passage from Vidyasagar's 'Sita's Exile' or from *Shakuntala*, he would try with extended arms to beg the reader to stop.

This old man was as much a friend of ours, as of my elder brothers and of my father. His age seemed suitable to all of us. It is not easy to get a more favourable listener for reading poetry aloud. Just as a cascade can dance merrily around the smallest boulder in its path, any occasion was enough for Srikantha-babu to be overwhelmed by his own mirth. I had composed a couple of paeans to the Almighty. As usual, I hadn't stopped to include worldly suffering and mortal pain. Srikantha-babu reasoned that such poetry was, in all respect, completely dedicated to the divine and if narrated to my father, he would be immensely pleased; with great enthusiasm he took the poems along to read aloud to my father. Fortunately I was not present there – but I got the news that my father had been very amused by the fact that the unbearable heat of the summer had affected his youngest son so early in the day as demonstrated by the poetry I had composed, and had burst out laughing. The sombre theme had not been able to influence him in the least. I am positive that if it were our superintendent Gobinda-babu, my composition would have earned due respect.

In singing, I was Srikantha-babu's favorite student. He often sang a traditional song: '*moye chhodo braja-ki bansuri* – torment me no more, O Braja's sweet flute'. He dragged me along from room to room to ensure that everyone at home had a chance to hear me sing this song. As I sang, he would pick up the tune on the strings of the sitar and each time I hit the notes '*moye chhodo*', he would join in and tirelessly work out the variations while nodding his head and locking gaze with the audience as though to prod them into liking the song.

He was my father's devoted friend. Based on a song in Hindi, he had composed a *Bramhasangeet*: '*Antaratara antaratam tini je/ bhulo na re tai* – the One who is innermost in you/ forget not His being'. Singing this song to my father, he would stand up from his seat, overwhelmed by emotion. He strummed the strings of his sitar and sang the first line, as though in question, "Who is the one innermost in you" – and followed up with a variation of the words of the song in answer, waving his hand in the direction of my father's face: "*Antaratara antaratam tumi je* – you are my innermost being."

When this venerable gentleman came to meet my father for the last time, my father was staying at his garden-villa on the banks of the Ganges at Chinsura. Srikantha-babu was terminally ill; he had no strength left to get up and was only able to see by prodding his eyelids open with his fingers. In this state, under his daughter's care, he travelled all the way from Raipur in Birbhum district to Chinsura. With great difficulty he managed to touch my father's feet once, before returning to his place of residence at Chinsura, where he breathed his last within the following few days. I heard from his daughter that lying on his death bed, he sang: "How sweet is your compassion, O Lord," before achieving complete silence forever.

The End of Bengali Lessons

WE WERE STUDYING Bengali in a class which was one year behind the scholarship class. At home, however, our Bengali lessons had progressed well beyond the requirements of the class. We had completed the book on physics by Akshay Kumar Dutta and also finished reading the epic poem, *Megnadbadh*. We studied physics without any connection with the material world; it was merely a bookish effort and our knowledge stayed at that level. It was time completely wasted. To my mind, it was more than a mere loss of time: if time is spent doing nothing, it is less of a loss, than if time is wasted in trying to do something. We were not comfortable reading the epic *Meghnadbadh* either. What is pleasurable to the senses would be rendered unpalatable if it is forced on the mind. If poetry is used to teach language, it is akin to shaving with a sword – not only is it demeaning to the sword, it is also hazardous to the throat. Poetry should be taught solely as poetry; using it as a short-cut to deliver lessons in vocabulary and grammar cannot please *Saraswati*, the Goddess of Learning.

At this stage, our ties with Normal School were suddenly severed. There is a little history behind it. A teacher from the school wished to read the biography of my grandfather in English, written by Kishori Mohan Mitra. My co-student and nephew Satyaprasad gathered up courage to go and ask for the book from my father. He felt that the normal Bengali we used in daily conversation would be inappropriate for the occasion.

Consequently, he used the traditional written form to express his request so faultlessly, that my father realised that in our zest to advance our knowledge of the Bengali language, we were on the path of losing our Bengali character. The next morning, as per our habit, just as we had spread our study table and hung the blackboard on the wall of the south veranda in anticipation of commencing our lessons with Nilkamal-babu - the three of us were summoned to the third floor chambers of my father. He declared, "From today, there is no need for you to study Bengali any further." Our hearts danced with joy.

Our tutor Nilkamal-babu was waiting for us downstairs; the book of geometry in Bengali lay open on the table and perhaps a repeat campaign on *Meghnadbadh* was being planned. Just as the typical demands of family life are meaningless at the time of death, the whole tableau including our tutor to the nail on the wall from which the blackboard was hung, seemed momentarily to us, as elusive as a mirage. How to break the news of our freedom to our tutor, with due solemnity, was the main challenge. We managed to control our emotions and conveyed the message. The strange lines and figures of geometry stared at us from the blackboard, while the epic, every word of which used to be an enemy, lay so helplessly on the table, that it was not hard to imagine it as a friend at that moment.

While taking his leave, our tutor said, "My duty demands that I deal with you harshly sometimes; don't keep those instances in mind. Later on, you will realise the value of what I taught you."

I have come to realise what he meant. Since I learnt Bengali from an early age, I was able to use my entire imagination effectively. As far as possible, getting educated should be like eating. The joy of taste commences from the very first bite and even before it is full, the stomach is alive with pleasure – consequently, its digestive enzymes cease to be idle. For the Bengali, such an experience is impossible with English education. At the first bite, there is a jolt to both rows of teeth – a minor earthquake seems to erupt within the mouth. Eventually, before one can come to terms with its cooked-in-syrup softness as compared to the initial hardness, half his age would be spent. Choked by spelling and grammar, he is overcome by countless tears of frustration as his inside stays hungry. In the end, when he is finally acquainted with the food, his hunger has died out. If opportunities to use the mind are lacking from the beginning, the mind begins to lose its speed of operation. Now that it is fashionable all over to teach English, I would like to pay my respects to departed sej-dada, my third elder brother, for his courage in arranging for our long-standing Bengali lessons against all odds.

We left Normal School and were admitted to Bengal Academy – an institution run by the British. This enhanced our prestige. We felt that we had grown up – at least we had climbed up one level in terms of freedom. As a matter of fact, whatever little progress we made at this school was in the field of freedom. Little did we follow what we were studying, we made no attempt to do so – and even when we did not, no one seemed to care. The boys here were rogues but not repugnant, and it was a great relief to me. One of them would ink the word 'ass' in English in reverse, on the palm of his hand and greet a fellow student with a 'hello' before applying a friendly slap to the back, thereby causing the name of the reviled creature to be inscribed on their victim's shirt; sometimes one would smack a peeled banana on a victim's head and disappear without a trace; at some other time, one would strike the boy in front on the head and then look away, posing innocence with a saintly face. These were mere physical pranks which left no mark on the mind – these were acts of mischief and not insult. I felt that I had managed to climb up from mire onto firm rock – I might skin my feet but I was saved from uncleanliness. One of the biggest advantages this school offered to boys like me was that no one harboured the impossible hope that we would improve in our studies. It was a small school with little income and we were on the principal's good books for paying our monthly fees regularly. Thus, Latin grammar did not become unbearable to us and out backsides remained uninjured, despite seriously neglecting our studies. I feel that this had more to do with the principal having forbidden the teachers to exercise their arms and less to do with their love for us.

There was nothing really annoying about this school, but the fact remains that it was nothing but a school. Its rooms were heartless, its walls were like prison guards – there was nothing homely about the place, it was merely a large compartmentalised box. There were no decorations anywhere, not a picture, no colours and there was nothing to attract a child's heart. The fact that children possess likes and dislikes did not matter to the school authorities. As a result, the moment a student stepped over the threshold into the narrow confines of the school, his mind grew demoralised and dejected – thus, I was never able to overcome the urge to flee from school.

I found a path to escape. My elder brothers had a home tutor for French – everyone called him Munshi – I have forgotten his true name. He was elderly and exceedingly lean. His appearance was like that of a skeleton enclosed in a mould of dark wax, without a trace of fluid or fat. Apparently, his knowledge of French was good and his English was passable, but he had no aspirations to fame whatsoever, in these fields. He believed that just as he was very skilful in show-fighting with a staff, he was extremely capable in music. Poised in our courtyard in bright sunshine he used to wave his staff about in a strange and menacing manner – his opponent being his own shadow. Needless to say, the shadow never won – and when he loudly proclaimed victory over his shadow after successfully beating it down with his staff and allowing himself a proud smile of victory – it lay at his feet in silence, pale and vanquished. Apparently his out of key singing sounded like a tune from hell – a nightmare that was a mixture of incoherent uttering and lament. Our singer Bishnu used to tease him sometimes, "Munshi-ji, you just robbed me of my bread" – he would not reply but he smiled with a dismissive expression on his face.

From the above, you can see that Munshi was not hard to please. Whenever we approached him, he would readily write an application to the school authorities requesting our leave of absence. The principal of the school did not worry too much about such applications because he knew very well, whether we attended school or not, would have little effect as such on the education system.

Now I have a school of my own and here, students commit all sorts of offences – it is the right of students to commit offences just as it is the right of teachers not to forgive. When we teachers, angered or scared by their behaviour, and worried about the welfare of the institution, contemplate strict punishment, then the rows upon rows of sins I committed in my student days come back to me, smiling in mockery at my face.

I realise well that we often measure children with the same scale as adults, forgetting that a child moves as fast as a cascade; if the water is tainted with an offence, there is no reason to be disheartened, since there is easy remedy for every fault in fluent movement; danger lurks where the flow stops, and it is there that we must be cautious. Thus, we have to be more worried about offences by teachers rather than those by students.

In order to enable us Bengalis to uphold our caste practices, we were given a lunch room to ourselves. We made friends with a few boys there. They were all elder to us. One among them was fond of *Raga Kafi* and he was even more fond of a particular person at his in-laws' place – as a consequence, he practiced the *raga* frequently and his other preoccupation too, continued unabated.

Another student merits a detailed description. His specialty was his excessive fondness for magic. He even went to the extent of getting a thin booklet published, giving himself, the author, the title of 'professor'. Before him, I had never beheld a student whose name appeared in print. Thus, I had a lot of respect, at least towards his knowledge of magic. I could not imagine anything false in the straight lines of printed words. Thus far, I had been taught by and influenced by printed matter, and so I had a special respect for it. One's writing in indelible ink was no small matter! There was no way to hide – one would have to stand straight and introduce himself to the world, all means of escape were cut off - such unmoving self-confidence was hard not to believe in. I remember well, maybe from the printing press of the *Bramosamaj* or from somewhere else, I managed to get hold of a few printing blocks containing some alphabets used to spell my name. I applied ink on the typeface and pressed the blocks to a sheet of paper; when the letters emerged, it was a most memorable event.

We used to take this author–classmate friend of ours, with us in our carriage, to school. This practice permitted him frequent access to our home. He was also pretty enthusiastic about acting and theatre. Once, with his help, we planted some bamboo posts and put up a stage in the wrestling arena, decorated by sheets of paper with pictures in myriad colours. I believe no performance on this stage was permitted due to orders from higher-ups.

However, we once performed a farce without a stage. It could be called, '*Bhrantibilas* – The Comedy of Errors'. Well, about the playwright, the readers have already been introduced to him to some extent. He is my nephew Satyaprasad. Whoever sees this calm and cultured gentleman today cannot possibly imagine what an expert Satya was, to engineer riots with ease, during his younger days.

The next episode is from a slightly later period in my life. I believe I was then twelve or thirteen years old. Our friend used to attribute such fantastic qualities to certain objects that I was stunned – I had a burning desire to put his words to test. Unfortunately, the objects were so rare that there were no means for me to lay my hands on them, other than by setting out in the footsteps of Sindbad the Sailor. However once, quite incautiously, the professor revealed a simpler technique rather than the usual extraordinary ones, and I was determined to test it out. Who knew, that if one were to apply gum from a certain herb onto a seed, it was possible to germinate it and cause the plant to grow fruit in the matter of an hour. However, it was not easy to disbelieve the words of a professor who had already published a book.

We pestered our gardener and managed to collect the herbal gum in sufficient quantity. We resolved to carry out the test on a mango pit, and so on a Sunday, we assembled on the third floor roof terrace to carry out our secret experiment.

I busied myself with applying the gum on the seed and trying to dry it in the sun – what kind of fruit resulted from the experiment, surely the mature readers will ask no more. But, I had no idea that during this one-hour period, in another corner of the terrace, Satya had grown an astonishing magical plant, complete with branches and leaves. The resulting fruits of his effort also proved to be equally bizarre.

After this incident, I did not realise for quite some time that the professor was consciously avoiding my company. He did not sit beside me in the carriage and he always seemed to keep a distance from me.

Suddenly, one afternoon in our study, he proposed: "Let us all jump down from this bench, one by one, and examine each other's technique." I thought that the professor had knowledge of many mysteries in life and maybe there was some deeper meaning to the jumping. All of jumped, including me. The professor uttered a deep-seated "Hmm", and nodded his head with seriousness. I implored him but got no clearer explanation.

One day, the magician said, "A few boys from a respectable household wish to make your acquaintance, and we must go to their place tomorrow." Our guardians did not find any reason to object and so off we went.

Curious people thronged the room. Everyone was eager to hear me sing. I sang a couple of songs. I was young then and my voice had not deepened to the lion's roar as it is now. Many in the crowd nodded and commented, "Indeed, what a sweet voice!"

After that, when we sat down to eat, we were surrounded by many people observing us. Prior to this occasion, I had very little experience of dining before strangers and I felt bashful. Besides, as I have already narrated, I was unable to eat sufficiently under the greedy stare of Iswar our domestic servant, and had developed a small appetite in the process. All the observers expressed surprise at my hesitant eating on that day. The way we, the invited guests, were examined by the hosts – if such observations were made compulsory and widespread, no doubt it would have benefited the development of life sciences in Bengal.

After a while, as a conclusion to the events, I received a couple of letters from the magician, whereupon everything became clear to me. Thereafter, the curtain fell on the entire episode.

Later I heard from Satya that during the process of generating magic within a mango seed, he had revealed to the professor that in order to avail the process of education, my guardians had sent me, an adult, to school disguised as a child. To all those interested in self-imagined scientific discussions, I have to say this: in the jumping test I had put my left foot forward – I did not realise on that day what a big mistake I had made.

My Father

EVER SINCE A few years prior to my birth, my father was engaged in frequent travel all over the country. During my childhood, he was almost a stranger to me. Sometimes he would come home quite suddenly, bringing a servant from another province along with him; we would be filled with eagerness to befriend these persons. Once a young Punjabi lad called Lenu came with him. We welcomed him with enthusiasm that would have been, in no way, less befitting for Maharaja Ranjit Singh-*ji* himself. He was from a distant land and that too a Punjabi to boot – thus he captivated our imagination. Just as I possessed great respect for Bhima and Arjuna of the epics, I held the Punjabi race in high esteem. They were warriors – though they had lost a few battles, I regarded such defeats as the fault of their opponents. My mind swelled with pride at having Lenu, a member of that race, in our midst. *Bouthakurani,* as I called my favourite sister-in-law, had a toy ship in a glass case that one could wind to make cloth waves swell up while the ship itself swayed to organ music. Though it took a lot of pleading to borrow this amazing object from *bouthakurani,* I would do so quite often in order to astonish this Punjabi youth. Since I was imprisoned at home, my mind was attracted to anything foreign, anything from a distant land. And thus, I was busy spending a lot of time with Lenu. For the same reason, Gabriel, a Jewish perfume seller who came clad in his customary robe with little bells, could move me very much; and the giant *Kabuli-wallah* in his loose soiled clothes and turban was a person of fearful awe in my eyes.

In any case, whenever father came home, we sated our curiosity from a distance by frequent visits to the living quarters of his servants. We could never reach him.

I can remember well that at some time during our childhood, an imminent attack on India by the Russian army – a perpetual bogey of the British government – was a topic of discussion on many lips. An overly helpful relative gave free rein to her imagination on the impending revolution, while describing it to my mother. My father had gone to the mountains at that time. It could not be said with certainty which secret pass the Russians would use to cross the Himalayas after penetrating Tibet, and emerge on the plains like a blazing comet. The eventualities filled her mind with dread. Surely no one else at home sympathised with her in her anxieties. Exhausted of all avenues of support from grown-ups, she finally turned to this child. She asked me, "Why don't you write a letter to your father informing him about the Russians?" Conveying my mother's worries, this was my first letter to my father. Not knowing how to write a letter or what to do, I sought the help of Munshi Mahananda in the office. No doubt the letter proved to be adequate. However, the language was redolent with the smell of old decaying paper on which the Goddess of Learning resided in a landlord's office of records. I received a reply to this letter. Father wrote to say that there was no cause for worry and he would drive away the Russians by himself. I am not sure whether my mother's fear of the Russians was in any way diminished by such strong reassurance, but my confidence in my father's abilities knew no bounds. After that, I used to present myself daily at Mahananda's office to write letters to him. Mahananda gave in to my pestering and prepared a few draft letters. But I had no means to pay for the postage. I used to think that once I handed over the letter to Mahananda, I no longer needed to worry about any further responsibilities and the letter would reach its destination easily. Needless to say, Mahananda was much older than me and these letters never reached the Himalayan foothills.

After days of travelling, when father returned to Kolkata to spend a few days at home, the whole house filled up and reverberated with his presence. I observed that the elders would put on proper attire, attend to personal appearance and spit out any betel that they may have had in their mouth, before coming to visit him. Everyone was cautious. My mother sat in the kitchen and personally attended to the cooking to prevent any shortcomings. Our old watchman Kinu stood at the gate in his tinselled turban and white uniform. We had been warned in advance not to disturb father by our running along the veranda. We walked slowly, we spoke gently; we were afraid to peek into his chambers.

Once, father came back from his travels to invest us with the sacred thread of the *brahmins*. With the help of an expert of the Vedanta, he personally compiled the rituals for the *upanayana* ceremony from Vedic-mantras. For many days, we sat in the courtyard and Becharam-babu had us practice to perfection, reciting mantras from the Upanishads which were compiled in the Book of the *Bramho*. The ceremony was performed following ancient Vedic methods, to the extent possible. With shaven heads and wearing ceremonial earrings, the three of us *brahmin* lads were locked into a room on the third floor for three days. We had great fun. We tugged at each other's earrings. There was a *baya* or the base drum of the *tabla,* lying on the floor of the room; standing on the veranda, when we glimpsed a servant passing by below, we beat on the drum, causing them to look up and see us; they lowered their gaze immediately in a mixture of guilt and worry and ran away. Thus, unlike novice monks at their guru's residence, we did not pass our days under very strict control. I believe that if one searched ancient hermitages, boys like us would not be hard to find; there is simply no evidence that they were much better persons than us. There is a tale of two young monks who spent entire days reciting verses from the Vedas and making oblations to the ceremonial fire; if such a story is truly narrated in the ancient holy books, I am not willing to take it at its face value, since the scripture called 'child's character' is older that all religious texts. No other as prominent a treatise has ever been written.

After attaining new *brahmin*-hood, we were very keen to silently recite the mystical *Gayatri mantra*. I tried the silent recitation taking special care to concentrate. I could not properly appreciate the significance of the verses at that age. I would focus on certain terms from the Sanskrit verses and try hard to stretch my mind around the words. I cannot express what I understood or what I thought then; it is certain though that understanding the meaning of words is not the most important thing for humans. The biggest part of education is not to explain, but to strike a chord in the mind. If a student is asked to describe what is it that has struck his mind so much, he can come up with a childish explanation at best. The impact to his mind is far deeper than what words can express; those teachers who drive students to be merely successful in examinations are not cognisant of the fact. I can remember that when I was young, I did not comprehend many things, but they touched me deep inside. As a very young child, on a cloudy day in the garden mansion at Mulajor beside the Ganges, I overheard my eldest brother reciting verses from the epic poem *Meghdoot*; I did not need to understand the words and nor did I have the means to – the happy and passionate rhythm of his narration was enough for me. Later in my childhood, when I knew very little English, I read completely a fully illustrated edition of 'The Old Curiosity Shop'. I could not understand most of it – certain vague images formed in my mind and I wove the pictures together with multi-coloured lengths of yarn from my imagination; in the hands of an examiner, no doubt I would have earned a big zero; but to me, the effort was definitely worth much more than zero. At another instance during my childhood, while touring in a boat on the Ganges with my father, among his other books I found an old copy of the *Geet Govinda* that had been published at Fort William. It was in Bengali script; the lines of poetry were not separated into verses; the lines were joined together inseparably as in prose. I had no knowledge of Sanskrit then. Since I knew Bengali well, I could understand the meaning of many words. I cannot say how many times I read that copy of the *Geet Govinda*. I understood little of what Jaydev the poet tried to convey, but the words and the rhymes commingled to weave an object in my mind that was not insignificant. There is a verse I remember which reads: 'There's a hut hidden away in the forest, where an early morn reveals the mystery of spring' – the beauty inherent in the picture excited my mind tremendously; the music and rhythm of the first few words, combined together in a form unique to Sanskrit, were enough to rouse me. Since this edition was published in a prose format, I had to decipher the diverse verses to discover their beauty – this was a very rewarding job for me. The day I was able to read the verse – 'Alas! Jewels adorn my physique, but I am tormented by flames fanned by my bereavement from you O *Hari*, I am filled with grief' – in the right meter, I was exhilarated. I did not completely understand Jaydev's poetry, nor was it something half-understood; my mind was overwhelmed by such beauty that I copied the entire *Geet Govinda* into a notebook. When I was older, I was smitten by lines from *Kumarsambhav*:

Mandakini-nirjhar-shikaranang
Bodha muhuh kampita-debdaruh
Yadbayu-ranbishta-mrigaih kiratai-
Rase-byate bhinna-shikhandi-barah.

When I read this *sloka* or Sanskrit verse, my mind filled with wonder. I did not grasp its meaning very much; just two descriptions: 'a stream cascades down from the mountain peak' and 'quivering leaves of *Debdaru*' captivated me; I longed to experience the flavour of the entire *sloka*. When my teacher explained the complete meaning, I was disappointed. The hunter is intent in the pursuit of a deer, while the wind tears apart the peacock plume of his headdress – such detailed depiction troubled me very much. I felt much better when I didn't follow entirely.

Anyone, who thinks back to their childhood days in some depth, will realise that conceiving everything clearly in entirety is not the most desirable thing. Traditional storytellers know this fact well and thus their narrations contain complicated Sanskrit words, which sometimes convey complex concepts that the listeners can only grasp a hint of, and never completely and clearly – this in itself is not of insignificant value. Those teachers, who look back and critically evaluate their past performance, often try to calculate whether what they delivered, have been fully grasped or not. Children and those not very highly educated, live in an initial heaven of knowledge, where it is not important to comprehend everything – and when they fall from grace, the grief of having to understand every meaning, dawns on them. However, this is also not the complete truth. In this world, the path, where rational understanding is not essential, is always the most significant. If this way is blocked, everyday life does not come to a standstill, but the means of reaching the ocean are barred and it is impossible to climb a mountain peak.

Thus as I mentioned earlier, at that age, it is not that I grasped the true significance of the *Gayatri mantra*, but there is something within the human mind that is satisfied even without complete comprehension. In this connection, I remember a day when I was seated on the floor in a corner of our study, silently reciting the *Gayatri mantra,* and my eyes profusely welled up with tears. I could not ascertain the cause of the tears. At that instance, if I were confronted by a strict examiner, I would have come up with a reason not connected in any way with the *Gayatri mantra*. The truth of the matter is that our intellect is not always informed of all that is going on within our mind.

The Journey to the Himalayas

AFTER THE SACRED thread ceremony, I became terribly worried about going to school with a tonsured head. Despite their attraction towards the bovine kind for a different purpose, the boys from the white race had no respect towards *brahmins*. As a result, even if they refrained from pelting our bare heads with other missiles, they were sure to rain ridicule and laughter on us.

During this time of torment, one day I got a call from the third floor. Father enquired whether I was interested in accompanying him to the Himalayas. If only I could have shouted "Yes I am," loud enough to reach the skies, my feelings would perhaps have found true expression. Bengal Academy versus the Himalayas – it was hardly comparable in any way.

Before starting on our journey, following his usual custom, my father called everyone at home to assemble in the courtyard to pray together; I sought the blessing of elders by touching their feet before getting into the train with my father. For the first time in my life, clothes had been tailored for me. Father had personally ordered the colour and the cloth. I also had a round velvet cap, embroidered with gold thread. It felt awkward worn on my shaven head, and so I held the cap in my hand. The moment we climbed into the carriage, father ordered, "Put it on your head."

There was no escaping from etiquette in front of my father. Though embarrassed, I had to put on the cap. Whenever I got a chance in the train, I would take it off. But it never escaped my father's attention. I had to place it back immediately.

Father was very meticulous in every thought and action of his, however big or small. He could not tolerate any concept to be hazy in his mind, and no action of his could ever be unplanned. His duties towards others, as well as those of others towards him were very well defined. As a nation, we are not particularly methodical. We do not count minor variations from plan to be worthy of consideration. As a consequence, all of us had to be fearful and cautious in our dealings with him. A slight deviation might not cause harm, but it adversely affected planning, and this hurt him. He visualised every part of his plan clearly in his mind. Thus, he planned every occasion down to the smallest detail – the relative position of objects, who would sit next to whom, who would be responsible for what – he did not let any part of the plan slip in any way. Afterwards, he had various people narrate the events to him. He then tried to piece the details together in his mind into a clear picture. In all this, he completely lacked the primary shortcoming of our national character. There was no place for tardiness in his planning, thinking, behaviour and conduct. Thus, during the journey to the Himalayas, on the one hand I enjoyed a lot of freedom, while on the other all my actions were inviolably predetermined. He did not interfere in the least when he granted me leave, but at the same time, he left no gaps in the rules he set for me.

It was planned that we stay at Bolpur for a few days at the beginning of our journey. Satya, my nephew I have introduced earlier, had been there some time ago with his parents. No child from a respectable household in the nineteenth century would believe the descriptions of the journey that he narrated to me. But in those days, I had not learned to recognise well the dividing line between the possible and the impossible. The ancient tomes by Krittibas or by Kasiramdas that we read were of no help in this regard. Illustrated children's books and magazines did not caution us beforehand about truth and falsehood. We came to terms with harsh reality only when we were exposed to the world.

Satya had declared that one needed special ability to get into a railway coach, one misstep and there would be no means of escape. Thereafter, when the train started, all of one's strength, had to be exerted to remain seated, otherwise the violent force of the moving train would cast him far away. I was very nervous upon reaching the station. However, I was able to climb into the coach with such ease that I began to wonder whether the main part of getting on a train was somehow yet to come. Afterwards, when the train started moving smoothly and there was no sign of impending danger, my mind filled with disappointment.

The train sped along; green fields bordered by bluish-green groves of trees and villages concealed in shadows, rushed by like two streams of pictures on either side of the train, as though in a torrent of mirages. We reached Bolpur in the evening. I shut my eyes as we were carried to our residence in a palanquin. I wished the wonders of Bolpur to unfold before my fully awake eyes the next morning – any introduction in the fading light of the day might spoil the undivided enjoyment stored for the next day.

I arose early the next morning and stepped outside with a nervously beating heart. My previous fellow-traveller had told me, that compared to other places in the world, Bolpur was unique in the sense, that though the path from the residential quarters to the kitchen was not covered by any roof, no rain or sunshine fell on the body. I set out to discover this astonishing path. I hope the readers will not be surprised to hear, that to this day, I remain unsuccessful.

Like other boys from the city, I had never before beheld rice paddies and after reading about cowherds in books, I had painted a charming picture of them in my imagination. I had heard from Satya that the paddies of Bolpur overflowed with grain, and that playing with the cowherds was a daily routine. Collecting rice from the paddies, cooking and partaking in a meal together with the cowherds, made up the highlights of the game.

Anxiously I looked around. Alas, in the surrounding rugged desert-like landscape there were no rice paddies! There might have been a cowherd or two out there somewhere, but there was no way to distinguish them as cowherds.

I lost little time in overcoming the regret at not seeing what I had hoped to – what I did perceive proved enough for me. The rule of the servants did not extend to Bolpur. The reigning deity of the arid expanse before me had drawn a blue boundary in the distant horizon, within which there was no obstruction to my free wandering.

Even though I was a mere child, my father never forbade my extensive wandering. At several places in the surrounding area, rainwater runoff eroded the sandy soil to levels below grade, and adorned by red pebbles and other types of stones, created small hill ranges, caves and caverns, rivers and streams that seemed to form the topography of a land of midgets. Such ravines with rounded hillocks are known as *khwai* in this region. From here, I used to collect different kinds of pebbles and stones and bring them to my father. He never belittled my perseverance, even for a day. He would express enthusiasm and say, "How wonderful! Where did you get all these?" I replied, "There are so many more! In thousands and thousands! I can bring some home every day." He then said, "That will be very good. You can decorate this hill with your collection."

An attempt to dig a pond was given up on account of the extremely hard ground. Soil from this unfinished excavation was piled high on the south side in the shape of a hill. Every morning, my father sat there on a chair and prayed. The sun rose in front of him from the eastern edge of the wilderness. He encouraged me to embed my stones on the sides of this hill. I was unable take along the heaped collection of pebbles and stones when we left Bolpur and I felt very sad. I did not realise then, that any load is a burden to be borne, and that there is a cost involved in freight; to this day, I find it difficult to accept, that having made a collection does not bestow me with the right to continue my relationship with it. If God had listened to my innermost prayer that day and had granted, 'Thou shalt bear the burden of these stones for thy entire life', perhaps I would not have been able to laugh at the matter today.

At one spot amidst the *khwai*, ground water seeped into a deep hole and collected there. Water overflowed an edge of the pool and flowed in a tiny stream through the sandy waste. Tiny fish swam against the current at the mouth of the stream in an act of daring. I went and told my father, "I found a beautiful source of water. We can get our supplies for drinking and bathing from there." He replied encouragingly, "Very well. That will indeed be great." As a reward to the explorer who had made the discovery, he arranged for water to be brought from the pool.

I used to roam the hills and valleys of the *khwai* whenever possible, in search of amazing wonders. I was the Livingstone of this tiny undiscovered territory. It was a country viewed in reverse through a telescope. Just as the streams and hills were diminutive, the wild *jamun* trees and date palm that grew there hesitantly were miniscule in equal measure. The fish in the stream of my discovery were just as minute, and their discoverer was no different.

I presume that in order to improve my sense of caution and responsibility, my father gave me a few coins for safekeeping and instructed, "You will have to keep count." He also entrusted me with the task of winding his valuable gold watch. He did not worry about the possibility of loss; rather my initiation to responsibilities was his primary motivation. He took me along during his morning walks. If we met any beggar, he would instruct me to give alms. In the end, when I sat down with him for bookkeeping, the accounts never tallied. One day, the balance remaining increased. He said, "I think I will have to appoint you as my cashier; my money multiplies in your hands." I took care to wind his watch daily. Perhaps the care was a bit too vigorous; in no time the watch had to be dispatched to Kolkata for repairs.

Here I am reminded of the time when I was older, and I had to present to my father the accounts for the areas under my responsibility. He used to live in Park Street then. On the second and third of every month I had to read aloud the accounts to him. He could no longer read himself. I had to present complete statements of accounts of the current month and compare with those of the previous month and previous year. He listened to the primary amounts and then did the calculations in his mind. If anything sounded unreasonable, he had the smallest sums read out aloud. On some days, if I tried to skip the part of the accounts where there were shortcomings in order to prevent his displeasure, the attempt would be futile; he perceived the overall statement of accounts clearly in his mind. If there were gaps he could catch them easily. Consequently, those two days of the month were especially worrisome. As I have already mentioned, it was his nature to clearly visualise to the smallest detail, whether it was a statement of accounts, or the landscape, or arrangements for a ceremony. He never saw the new temple at Shantiniketan or many other things there with his own eyes. However, when people went to meet him after visiting Shantiniketan, he would not rest until he had drawn a complete picture in his mind of the things unseen, by listening to their descriptions. His memory and his power of comprehension were exceptional. Whatever he accepted into his mind, could not be corrupted.

His favourite *slokas* were marked in his copy of the *Bhagavat Gita*. He had me copy these out, complete with Bengali translation. At home, I was a boy of no importance; over here, I basked in the glow of being entrusted with important responsibilities.

Meanwhile, I bade farewell to the blue notebook and acquired a hardbound copy of the Letts diary. Nowadays, in order to give poetry due respect, attention is being directed towards the use of proper notebooks and other accompaniments. The attempt is not just to write poetry, but to establish oneself as a poet before one's own imagination. Thus, when I composed poetry at Bolpur, I loved to sit sprawled on the ground, below a young coconut palm at the boundary of our garden and to fill my notebook. This seemed very poet-like to me. Seated on the gravelly ground which was bereft of a blade of grass, bathed in the heat of the sun, I had composed a heroic epic poem titled 'Prithviraj's Defeat'. All its spirit of courage and bravery was not able to protect this poem from extinction. Its able vehicle, the hardbound Letts diary too disappeared without a trace, in the footsteps of her elder sister, the blue notebook.

Starting out from Bolpur, we stopped to rest at stations like Sahibgunj, Danapur, Allahabad and Kanpur before finally reaching Amritsar.

An incident occurred during our journey that is still etched very clearly in my mind. The train had stopped at some station. The ticket examiner came and checked our tickets. He looked at my face. It seemed as though he suspected something but dared not speak out. A little later, he came back with another official; they hesitated outside the door of our carriage for a while, and then went away. For the third time, perhaps it was the stationmaster, who presented himself before us. He examined my half-ticket and asked my father, "Is this boy not more than twelve?" My father replied, "No". Then I was eleven. I must have grown faster than my age. The stationmaster declared, "You will need to pay a full fare for him". Father's eyes blazed with anger. He immediately gave them money from his case. When they came back to return the change, he flung the coins back at them which scattered all over, after impacting the stone platform with ringing sounds. The stationmaster cowered and retreated; father hung his head low in insult for being suspected of the lowly act of lying to save money.

I can remember the *gurdwara* at Amritsar as though in a dream. On many mornings while walking with my father, I had been to the Sikh temple located in the middle of the lake. Devotional chanting and singing went on for the whole day. Father sat in the midst of the Sikh worshippers in the temple and suddenly broke into a tune and joined in their singing; hearing their hymns from the lips of a foreigner caused much excitement among the locals who embraced him with open arms. He returned with a chunk of sugar candy and other sweet offerings.

Once, father invited home a singer from the temple ensemble, and listened to his rendering of devotional songs. I presume that an award of lower value, than what was given to the singer, would have sufficed to make him happy. As a result however, the number of those wishing to sing for us at home grew to such an extent that we were forced to take strict measures to block their path. Unable to make headway at home, they started accosting us on government roads. Every evening, my father used to take me along for a walk. At these times, singers continued to appear one after the other, each with a *tanpura* slung across his shoulder. Just as a bird which is not unfamiliar with hunters gets alarmed at the sight of a gun-barrel on a shoulder, the very sight of the tip of a *tanpura* reduced us to a similar state of mind. But the quarry grew so wary, that the droning of the *tanpura* worked like a blast from an empty round; it served to drive us farther away and never caused us to succumb.

As the shadows lengthened into evening, father used to come and sit on the veranda facing the garden. I would then be called to sing *Brahmasangeet* in his presence. The moon has risen, its radiance filters through the branches of trees and illumines the veranda as I sing in *Behag* –

"Who, but you can deliver us from our troubles,
Who else, but you, is our saviour from darkness?"

Father listened in silence with his head bowed and palms on his lap clasped in prayer – I can still recollect a clear picture of that evening.

I have mentioned earlier how father had laughed, as I encouraged by Srikantha-babu, recited two of my devotional compositions. I was able to exact revenge for that, much later in life. I would like to bring up that incident in this context.

Once, during the day of the *Magh* festival, I composed several songs in the morning and in the evening. One among those is –

Eyes cannot behold your greatness,
for you reside within every eye.

Father was at Chinsura during that period. Jyoti-dada and I were sent for to his place of residence. He had Jyoti-dada sit with the harmonium and asked me to sing all of my latest compositions one by one. Some songs, I even had to sing twice.

After the singing was over he said, "If the king of the country knew the language of the land and recognised the importance of literature, he would have surely rewarded poets. Since there is no possibility of that happening from the king's end, it falls upon me to do the job." And having said that, he handed me a cheque for rupees five hundred.

Intending to teach me English, my father took along with us, several volumes of Peter Parley's Tales. From these, he chose the biography of Benjamin Franklin for my lessons. He felt that the narrative would read like a story and I would benefit from reading it. However, he realised his mistake while making me read it. No doubt, Benjamin Franklin had been a very intelligent man. It was the calculative and utilitarian narrowness of his religious principles that troubled my father. He grew irritated by examples of Franklin's earthy wisdom and advice and could not refrain from speaking out.

Prior to this, my reading of Sanskrit had been limited to the primers. Father started teaching me higher level grammar and instructed me to memorise word forms for vocabulary. Our Bengali lessons had been so exhaustive, that in the process, our Sanskrit education had also progressed quite far. Right from the start, father encouraged us to use Sanskrit words to the maximum extent. From whatever I read, I rearranged words and conjugated them with endings appropriate to Sanskrit and turned the divine language to a tongue of the devil. But father never laughed at my acts of daring.

Apart from this, he would explain many topics from Proctors' easy-to-read text on astrology and I translated these into Bengali.

Among the books he took along on the trip for his own reading, there was a particular one that aroused my curiosity very much. It was Gibbon's Rome in ten to twelve large hard-bound volumes. Looking at them, I did not feel the contents to be the least interesting. While I was forced to read a lot of things because I was but a young boy, I used to wonder why he took the trouble, when he was not answerable to anybody and could do as he pleased.

We stayed at Amritsar for about a month. Towards the end of the month of *Chaitra,* we started for the hills of Dalhousie. I was finding it impossible to pass my time at Amritsar. The call of the Himalayas was making me impatient.

As we were being carried uphill on litters, the plateaus and valleys around us were aflame with the beauty of myriad spring crops in line after line of cultivated tracts, stacked level by level. Every day we started our journey early after a breakfast of bread and milk, and stopped to rest at the end of the day in a *dak-bunglow*. There was no rest for my eyes during the day and my mind worried lest I overlooked something. Tucked in the corner of the mountains, at some bend in the path where tall trees cast deep shadows, and where a stream or two emerged from cool hidden recesses of the forest over dark moss covered rocks to cascade gently down at the feet of meditating ascetics like their playful daughters in attendance, the bearers set our litters down and rested. As I absorbed my surroundings greedily, the thought of leaving such an alluring place behind, filled me with dismay and I longed to linger.

This is the advantage of new acquaintance. The mind fails to realise that there is more to follow. If it did, the calculative mind would try to save some of the attention for later. Only when the mind realises that everything is rare and priceless, does it overcome its habitual miserliness and apportions due value. Thus, on some days, I imagine myself to be a foreigner while travelling along the streets of Kolkata. Then I realise that we miss out seeing a lot of things out there for failing to realise their significance. It is for this reason that people travel to foreign lands to satisfy their hunger for observing new things.

My father entrusted me with the responsibility of the safekeeping of his cash-box. There was no reason for him to believe that I was the ablest person for the task. The box contained a lot of money meant for our travels. He would have had greater peace of mind had he handed over the box to Kishori Chatterjee, but perhaps his objective was to give me a sense of responsibility. One evening, on reaching the *dak-bunglow,* he reprimanded me when I kept the cash-box on the table instead of handing it over to him.

When we reached a *dak-bunglow*, my father would pull a chair outside and sit down. As evening fell and the stars grew bright in the clear mountain sky, he identified for me together the heavenly bodies with their astrological significance.

At Bakrota, our residence was located on a mountain peak. Though it was the early summer month of *Baisakh,* the cold had not yet abated. Moreover, along pathways, snow untouched by sunshine had not yet melted.

Even over here, father never stopped my unchecked wandering, anticipating danger of any kind.

An expanse of thickly wooded forest lay on a lower plateau. I frequented these woods, taking along an iron tipped staff. The trees towered above me like giants, casting massive shadows - their vast lives spanning, who knows how many hundreds of years. A tiny human child born just the other day, moved freely among them, rubbing against their trunks and yet they could not utter a word. I experienced a strange feeling the moment I entered the half-dark space of the forest. It felt like the cold touch of a reptilian skin; and on the forest floor, stacked with heaps of fallen leaves, the interplay of light and shadow seemed to create a variegated pattern like that on the back of a gigantic reptile.

My bedroom was situated at one end of the building. From my bed, through the glass panes, in the indistinct starlight, I could perceive the pale yellowish glow emanating from snow clad peaks. On some days, I do not remember how late at night, I observed my father silently walking by with a lantern in his hand, his body wrapped in a red shawl. He was on his way to the glass covered veranda in the front of the house for his prayers.

At sunrise, my father drank a bowl of milk at the end of his prayers; and then he had me stand beside him as he recited verses from the Upanishad in prayer once more.

After that, he took me along for a walk. How could I possibly keep up with him when many grown-ups would have found it difficult to do so? I broke off midway, and following steep mountain paths, climbed my way home.

After father returned there was an hour of English lessons. This was followed by a bath in cold snow-melt water at ten o'clock. There was no escape from this; the servants dared not disobey his orders and mix hot water in the urn containing bathing water. As encouragement, he used to narrate stories about bathing in unbearably cold water in his youth.

Drinking milk was another act of perseverance for me. My father drank copious quantities of milk. I am not confident whether I could have inherited his milk drinking prowess. But my eating and drinking took a reverse direction for reasons I have already narrated earlier. I had to drink milk with him always. I sought the help of our servants. Out of pity towards me or maybe due to their affection for me, they started filling my bowl with more froth than milk.

After the midday meal, father sat down once again to impart lessons. But it used to prove impossible for me. The sleep lost at dawn returned with vengeance. My body drooped over repeatedly, overcome by sleep. Out of sympathy toward my condition, father stopped the lessons and my sleep vanished almost immediately. Thereafter, it was the time to answer to the call from the Lord of the Mountains.

On some afternoons, with my staff in hand, I climbed one mountain peak after another; my father was not worried of the fact. I have observed right up to the end of his life that he never wanted to place any obstacle on the path of our freedom. We have gone against his taste and wish on many occasions; if he wanted, he could have prevented us, but he never did. He waited patiently, expecting us to do our duty from our hearts. He was not satisfied that we accept truth and beauty from the outside; he knew well that unless one loved truth, there was no way to accept truth. He also knew that it might be possible to return to truth even if one strayed afar, but once subjugated under strict control, all paths to truth would be closed forever.

At the start of my youth, I had a whim of attempting a journey to Peshawar by the Grand Trunk Road, on a bullock cart. The proposal met with disapproval all round and there were valid reasons for that. But when I approached my father, he said, "That's a great idea; railway travel is hardly any travel at all." Having said that, he went on to expand on how he had walked, ridden a horse drawn carriage or used many other means of conveyance during his travels. He did not express any possibility of danger or difficulty I might have to face.

At another instance, when I had been appointed as the new secretary of the Aboriginal Society, I went to his Park Street residence and declared, "I do not like it at all that only a *brahmin* can be a priest in the *Adi-Brahmosamaj* and not a person from any other caste." He replied at once, "Very well, please find a remedy if you can." But after getting his permission, I realised that I lacked the power to redress the situation. I could perceive incompleteness, but could not create the opposite. Where were the people? I did not possess the strength to call upon the right persons. Nor did I have the ingredients to reconstruct what I was planning to bring down. My father felt that any binding norm was good until the right people came forward on their own to disown it. However, not for a moment did he dissuade me by talking about hurdles in the path of my aspirations. Just as he let me wander unimpeded in the hills and the mountains, he granted me the independence to choose my own destinations in my quest for truth. He had not been afraid that I would make a mistake, nor did he worry that I would hurt myself. He held up an ideal of life before our eyes, but he never raised the rod of control.

During our travel, I discussed household matters with my father quite often. The moment I received a letter from home, I rushed to show it to him. Surely, he must have got the picture of many things from me that he could not possibly have had from anyone else.

If he received any letters from my two elder brothers, he would let me read them. This proved to be my education on how to write letters to him. To my father, lessons in such ways and means of the world were very essential in life.

I remember well that mej-dada, my second elder brother, had written in a letter, how the collar around his neck had transformed into a halter as he slogged it out in his place of work – father asked me to explain the meaning of certain lines from that passage. He did not like my explanation and put forth one of his own. But such was my audacity at that moment that I dared to differ. I argued with him at length. If it had been anyone else, I would have been stopped in my tracks with a rebuke; but he withstood my protests with patience and tried to reason with me.

He told me many entertaining stories. I heard several tales from him about the extravagance of the rich of those days. The border on the cloth from Dhaka – renowned for its soft texture – seemed coarse to the refined gentlemen of the day and so they wore their dhotis with the borders ripped out; such stories I heard from him. To prevent the milkman from adding water to milk, a servant was appointed; to oversee the work of this servant a supervisor was appointed, and in this fashion the number of servants kept multiplying just as the colour of milk turned murkier and the quality impossible to tell. When queried by the babu, the milkman replied that if the number of supervisors increased any further, a manifestation of cockles, snails, and shrimps in the milk was inevitable. When I heard this story from his lips for the first time, I had been very amused.

After spending a few months with him in this way, my father sent me back home to Kolkata along with his trusted aide, Kishori Chatterjee.

Homecoming

THE RESTRICTIVE CONTROL I was under earlier broke down completely during my journey to the Himalayas. After I returned, I was able to establish my authority. One who is under constant surveillance is barely noticed; only after going out of sight and then coming back, I was able to capture everyone's attention.

My good fortune commenced during the railway journey back home. I was a young boy with a sequined headgear, travelling alone with just an attendant; an abundance of healthy living had given certain robustness to my frame. All European ladies and gentlemen who got into the railway car, could not refrain from showering affection on me.

It was not just a case of returning home after a lengthy period of travel in foreign lands – it was coming out of exile that I had been subject to for so long, even while residing at home, and entering inside. Obstacles in the path leading to the inner chambers disappeared; I could no longer be confined to the servants' quarters. I captured a good deal of attention in the assembly held in my mother's chambers. I garnered a lot of love and affection from my then youngest sister-in-law.

In childhood, a man gets love and care from women, even without asking. Just as he needs air and water for survival, women's affection is equally essential for his existence. However, no one feels for the light and air that sustain us; similarly, it is natural for children to take the affection from women-folk for granted. On the contrary, children are often impatient to cut off the strands of such caring nets and be free. If a man does not get his hands on what he is entitled to, he craves for it. Such was my condition. Being thus far reared by servants in their quarters, and then suddenly thrust into the profuse affection of women, I could no longer keep in check the thought of what I had been missing. As a child, when the inner chambers were out of bounds, I imagined my inner dream world to be located in there. I perceived the place that was barricaded from me to be the one which offered release from all bondage. I thought that there were no schools there, no teachers, and no one was coerced into doing anything against his wishes; one's secret leisure would be full of mystery, he would not have to account for every moment of his day to someone else and he could spend his time in play as he desired. In particular, I observed that chor-didi, the youngest of my elder sisters who studied with us under Nilkamal *panditmosai*, was not controlled by any disciplinary ruling like the rest of us. At ten o'clock, we ate hurriedly and got ready for school like obedient children, while she walked indoors contentedly swinging her braids; thus seeing her go, hurt me very much. After that, when a new bride arrived at home wearing a golden necklace, the mystery surrounding the inner chambers further deepened. I longed to befriend the woman who came from far beyond, and yet was a part of our family now; one with whom I was not acquainted in the least, but who was now a close relation. However, if I managed to reach her on some pretext, chor-didi chased me out exclaiming, "What are you doing here, go on, go outside!" Then, disappointment on one hand, and insult on the other, caused much pain in my mind. Moreover, through the glass panelled doors of their cupboards, I caught glimpses of valuable objects of glass and porcelain – in myriad colours and varied decorations! We were never allowed to touch these objects; we never dared to ask. But these exceptional and beautiful wonders, served to further render the unreachable inner chambers, in rare colours.

In this manner, I spent my days always at a distance, prevented from coming closer. Just as nature outside maintained its distance from me, so also did the inner chambers of my home.

Consequently, whatever little I could see stayed in my mind as pictures. After nine o'clock in the evening, having completed lessons from Ahgar *mastermosai*, we are on our way to bed in the inner portion of the house; we cross the long hallway that is enclosed by blinds in the dim light of a flickering lantern, take a few steps down in the semi-darkness to enter the inner veranda that encloses a courtyard, from the western end of the veranda a moonbeam slants in, the opposite sides are cloaked in darkness, the maids of the house sit side by side in that strip of moonlight with their legs outstretched as they roll wicks for lamps on their thighs while conversing softly in their regional dialect – many such pictures are etched permanently in my mind. Afterwards, we would complete our evening meal, wash our feet in the outer veranda and then the three of us would climb onto a large bed and lie down – a servant named Shankari or Pyari or Tinkori would come and sit on the ground at the head of the bed and narrate the adventures of a prince travelling across extensive and desolate lands, and when the stories ended silence would take over the bedroom; as I turned to face the wall, in the dim light I would see that patches of plaster had flaked off at some places, creating myriad lines and patterns in black and white; I would interpret the patterns into many kinds of fantastic pictures as I fell asleep; thereafter, at midnight on some days, I would hear the loud cries of caution from old Swarupsardar as he walked from one veranda to the next, keeping guard.

One day, from the little known inner chambers that were coloured by my imagination, I received long awaited affection. What would have been easy to accept, if only it had been received regularly in moderate quantities, I am not sure whether I was able to bear the burden of receiving the same substance in its entirety, in such an unexpected manner.

The tiny traveller spent some days after his return, narrating tales of his travels in room after room. Repeated telling caused clashes in imagination, which in turn resulted in the narrative becoming so loose that it was impossible to link it to the description of the actual incident. Alas, like all other things, stories grow old and turn pale, and the collection of wonder in the tales wears thin. The more old tales lose their shine and begin to dim, the more they need to be coloured with a new coat of paint.

After returning from my sojourn in the hills, I earned the position of the main speaker in the assembly convened by my mother, while she sought fresh air on the roof terrace. It is difficult to resist the temptation to try to be famous in front of one's own mother, while it is not difficult to achieve the fame in her eyes.

While studying at the Normal School, when I discovered that the sun is one million and four hundred thousand times larger than the earth, I declared the fact in my mother's assembly. This was proof, that what appeared small, could in fact, be much larger. I recited from my memory, poems from our language and grammar primer, that were cited as examples of poetic expression, and astounded my mother. I still remember one of those –

O fly, my dear!
With what gentility thou doth, and hold your hands both,
But why do you display your many sharp feelers?

Whatever knowledge I acquired in those days from Proctor's volume on stars and planets, I inflicted on the hapless audience of the evening assembly, who had come out merely to be caressed by the soft south breeze on the roof terrace.

My father's personal attendant, Kishori Chatterjee was an erstwhile singer of a group which sang *panchali* or folk songs with a religious undertone. While we were in the hills, he used to say, "Oh dadaji, if only I can have you with me, we can form an incomparable *panchali* troupe." I was very tempted – accompanying an itinerant team of *panchali* singers and singing songs from different lands seemed a great privilege. I learnt many songs from Kishori which filled our gatherings with fervor that was not possible when I described the sun's fiery character or Saturn's cold brilliance.

Most people live their entire lives reading the *Ramayana* only in its Bengali version as written by Krittibas. I managed to startle my mother more than anyone else for having read the original version in Sanskrit as composed by *Maharshi* Balmiki, during the stay with my father. She was very pleased and said, "*Accha*, my child, why don't you read us a bit from that *Ramayana*?"

Alas, it was but a piece from the Sanskrit reader and moreover my understanding of it was very limited; when I started reading, I realised that several passages were no longer clear to me as though I just suffered a loss of memory. But my mother was already impressed with my intellectual prowess as she sat waiting eagerly to experience the joy of listening to the true Ramayana in my voice; I did not have the strength to disappoint her by a mere, 'I have forgotten'. As a result, there were considerable gaps between my reading of the text of the epic as composed by Balmiki, and my interpretation thereof. I am sure *Maharshi* Balmiki in heaven, forgave the offence of an immature child seeking fame in his own mother's eyes, in good humour and with an affectionate smile. However the slayer of vanity *Madhusudan*, or Lord Krishna in another form, did not let me off so easily.

My mother felt that I had achieved the unattainable; so in order to surprise others in equal measure she said, "Let's hear you read it out to Dwijendra." I sensed great danger and protested strongly. Mother paid no heed. She called for bar-dada or my eldest brother. No sooner than he had arrived that she declared, "Rabi has learnt to read from Balmiki's Ramayana; just listen to him once." I had to obey. Kind *Madhusudan* pardoned my trespass this time, after a mere hint of his power to strike vanity down. Bar-dada was perhaps preoccupied in some composition of his and he displayed little inclination to hear out my Bengali interpretation. He sat and listened to a few *slokas*, remarked 'very well done' and promptly left.

After this, it became all the more difficult for me to continue going to school. I worked out several schemes and started escaping from Bengal Academy. We were admitted to St. Xavier's next, but it was of no use.

My elder brothers tried to remedy the situation several times before giving up on me completely. They even stopped their admonitions. One day bar-didi, my eldest sister said, "We were all very hopeful that you will turn out to be a great man when you grow up, but now every hope has been dashed to the ground." I realised well that my position in civilised society was being downgraded constantly, but I could not come to terms with schools far removed from life and its beauty all around, where each institution was a heartless and nightmarish combination of prison and hospital, grinding relentlessly on.

From St. Xavier's, I have a pleasurable memory that has persisted clearly to this day – it is the memory of the teachers there. All our teachers were not of the same type; there were one or two especially in our class, in whom I failed to perceive, the deep humility of the believer. Instead, they had not been able to rise much higher than the usual teachers produced by the education factory, who troubled their students. The education mill is a large one and on top of that, there is no stronger vice in the world to crush the human heart and spirit than superficial religious practices. There are many who have not been able to advance further than observance of religion merely from the outside, and if these people become cogs in the wheel of education, the product cannot be expected to be of high quality; a few among our teachers were perhaps good examples of such people. However, I do have a memory that influenced my mind, which holds high the ideal in the lives of all the teachers of St. Xavier's. We did not have much to do with Father D. Peneranda; presumably he had come as a replacement for one of our regular teachers. He was a Spanish national. His English pronunciation was laboured. Maybe it was for this reason that students failed to pay much attention to him. I think, he used to feel the impact of the indifference among the students, which he politely tolerated day after day. I do not know why, but I felt for him. He was not handsome but he held a strange attraction for me. Just by looking at him, it seemed that his mind was engaged in perpetual worship, his being was pervaded by God's greatness from within and by a deep solitude. We had a half-hour class to write a composition and I usually sat pen in hand, distracted by fleeting ideas. One day, Fr. Peneranda was the teacher during this class. He kept walking between the benches. He must have noticed a few times that my pen barely moved. Once he stopped behind me, stooped and gently placed a hand on my back and asked in a soft affectionate tone, "Tagore, are you not feeling well?" There is nothing special about this but I have not forgotten his question to this day. I cannot speak for the other students, but I caught a glimpse of a great mind inside him; whenever I recollect the incident, I am able to gain entry into a quiet and hidden temple of God.

At the same time there was an old teacher whom the students loved very much. His name was Fr. Henry. He used to teach in the higher classes and I did not know him very well. I remember one aspect of him that is worth mentioning. He knew Bengali. Once he asked a boy in his class Nirad, the derivation of his name. Nirad had always been a self-assured type and he had never been much concerned about the derivation of the word which was his name, and which meant cloud; thus he was caught on the wrong foot. But then he reasoned that there were so many big and unfamiliar words in the dictionary and to be unable to find a suitable derivation for his own name – which in fact did not exist – would be akin to an accident of being run over by one's own carriage; Niru thus coined an instant derivation and glibly replied, "*Ni* or negation of *rad* or sunshine equals *nirad;* implying that *nirad* is what that causes sunshine to be snuffed out of the sky."

Studying at Home

GYANCHANDRA BHATTACHARYA MAHASAY, the son of Anandachandra Bedantabagis was our tutor at home. When he could no longer tie me down to studies required by my school, he gave up and devised new methods. He started teaching me *Kumarsambhav* by translating into Bengali from Sanskrit. He also started explaining Macbeth and until I had managed to set the translation to a Bengali poetical form, he would lock me in the study. I completed translating the whole book. Fortunately, it got lost in the way and as a result, the burden of the fruits of my labour, are less by a corresponding proportion.

Ramsarbasya Pandit-mahasay had the onerous duty of imparting knowledge of Sanskrit to us. He finally gave up the impossible task of teaching grammar to his unwilling students and started breaking down *Shakuntala* into Bengali for us. In order to have me read out my translation of Macbeth to Vidyasagar Mahasay, he took me along with him to see the learned man. When we reached the place, Rajkrishna Mukhopadhyay was also present. I entered the book-lined study with trepidation in my heart; I cannot say that Vidysagar's face bolstered my confidence in any way. I had never before had an audience with as great a person; thus, I must have yearned strongly for acclaim at the occasion. I think I was able to return home with a certain amount of encouragement. I can recollect that Rajkrishna-babu had advised me to set apart the speech of witches from that of other characters by its strangeness of language and rhythm.

During our childhood, the body of available literature in Bengali was rather frail. I think I must have completed all books worth reading, or otherwise. In those days, books for children were not set apart from those for adults. That did not affect us very much. Books for children today are so diluted in form and content, that they are merely consolation in the name of literature and wherein they regard children to be merely childish creatures and not as human beings. There ought to be some kind of understanding, that children when they read books, will understand some parts, and fail to understand others. In our childhood, we read voraciously; what we understood and what we did not, both had impact on our minds. The world works on children's mind in a similar fashion. Whatever they are able to internalise is no doubt their gain; what they fail to do so also contribute to their progress.

When a farce on marital affairs by Dinabandhu Mitra Mahasay was published, we were not old enough to be permitted to read that. A distant relation at home was reading the book. I begged her to let me read it, but to no avail. She used to keep the book locked in a chest in her room. Thus obstructed, my determination hardened and I warned her, "I will read this book somehow."

In the afternoon, while she sat playing a game of flash, the keys to the chest were knotted to the *anchal* end of her sari behind her.

I was never interested in cards; in fact I was particularly averse to the game. But on that day, it would have been difficult to imagine that. I sat still as a picture, watching the game with feigned interest. When the game was about to reach a climax and everyone was engrossed in the proceedings, I tried to untie the keys from her sari. But my fingers lacked the dexterity required for the task, and I was too excited in my eagerness; I was caught. The owner of the keys laughed and swung forward the end of her sari to which the keys were tied, so that these now rested on her lap, and then she turned back to the game.

I devised a scheme. This relation of mine was addicted to chewing tobacco. I managed to get hold of a box with betel leaves and chewing tobacco and I kept it in front of her. The event turned out to be just as I had hoped. She had to get up to spit out the betel juice from her mouth. Just as she did so, the bunch of keys tied to the end of her sari fell from her lap onto the ground, whereupon, as was her habit, she flung the *anchal* of her sari over her shoulders, until the keys once gain hung behind her. This time the keys were stolen and the thief avoided detection. The book was read. Thereafter, I returned the keys with the book to the rightful owner and saved myself from the punishment as per law, for stealing. The lady tried to scold me, but it was not as strongly worded as expected; she was amused from within and similar was my condition.

Rajendralal Mitra Mahasay used to bring out an illustrated monthly publication on a variety of topics. There was a bound volume of these magazines in my third elder brother or sej-dada's cupboard. I managed to get hold of that. I still remember the pleasure of reading the book several times. With the big square volume resting on my chest, I have spent many a holiday afternoon lying on my bed, reading about the narwhal, or amusing stories about judgment meted out by a *kazi*, or provincial judge or novels about Krishnakumari.

I wonder why we no longer have such publications. Present day papers are filled with science, philosophy and archaeology on one hand, while on the other with numerous short stories, poetry and insignificant travel writing. I am yet to see a paper of medium standard, suitable for easy reading by the majority of the people.

In England, most publications like Chambers Journal, Castle's Magazine and Strand Magazine are dedicated to serving the masses. These publications are successfully able to convert highbrow knowledge to a form suitable for consumption by the masses. It is knowledge in this simplified form that is very useful to most people.

In my childhood, I was acquainted with another small magazine. It was called *'Abodh-bandhu'*, or 'Friend of the Less-knowing'. I used to borrow unbound copies of this magazine from my eldest brother or bar-dada's shelf on many days and finish reading them, sitting near the open door of his south facing room. I first read poems by Biharilal Chakrabarty in this publication. It was his poetry, among all others, that captivated my heart the most, in those days. The poems were like songs from the fields and the woods set to simple tunes on the flute that rang out in my mind. I shed countless tears after reading the stories of Paul and Virginia in this magazine in lively translation. O where lies that beach by the sea! Where are the rows upon rows of coconut palm, swaying in the ocean's breeze! Where is the mountain, whose slopes are dotted with grazing goats! In the sun dappled afternoons, on a south facing veranda of Kolkata, what sweet mirage unfolded! And what romance played out on the dark forest trails of that desolate island between Virginia – the girl with a colourful scarf covering her head - and a young Bengali lad!

At last, Bankim's *'Banga-darshan'*, or 'A vision of Bengal' appeared on the horizon and successfully captured the hearts of all Bengalis. Firstly, I had to wait eagerly for the end of the month for the next issue to arrive; and when it did, I had to wait for the elders to finish reading first, which was all the more unbearable to me. About *'Bishbrikhya* – The Poison Tree' and *'Chandrasekhar'* - nowadays anyone can read these at one stretch with ease; but for month after month, the way we desired, waited, and caused the reading of a few fleeting hours to resonate in our minds during the long periods of waiting in between, enabled us to prolong our reading over many days, causing gratification to be coupled with dissatisfaction and enjoyment with the thirst to know further – no one will ever enjoy such an opportunity again.

I coveted the compilation of poetry from ancient times by Srijukta Sadacharan Mitra and Akshay Kumar Mahasay. My guardians subscribed to the publication but were not regular readers. Thus, it was not a difficult task for me to collect these together.

The difficult and distorted lyrics of Vidyapati in *Mythili* dialect were all the more attractive to me because of their obscurity. Rather than depend on the commentary, I tried to understand by myself. Wherever a difficult word was used repeatedly, I noted each usage in a little hard bound notebook. I also noted down the special grammar usages to the best of my ability.

The Atmosphere at Home

DURING MY CHILDHOOD, one of the greatest opportunities for me lay in literary winds that blew through my home day and night. I can remember that as a child, I would stand still for hours on certain evenings, holding onto the veranda railing. In the outer visitor's hall in front of me, there would be bright lights, the presence of many people, and large carriages at the doorway. I did not quite understand what was going on, I just stood in the darkness, staring at the bright strings of light. Though the separating gap was not really large, the lights were far away from my childhood world. My elder cousin Gyanendra or Gana-dada was then engaged in directing a new play that he had Ramnarayan Tarkaratna compose for him. Their enthusiasm for literature and for the performing arts knew no bounds. They were trying to welcome the new age of enlightenment in Bengal in every possible way. In their dress and appearance, poetry and music, fine arts and performing arts, religion and politics of freedom and in every other aspect of life and culture, their minds were filled with nascent nationalistic ideals. Gana-dada specially loved discussing the history of every country on Earth. A historical play on Emperor Vikramaditya written by him had been published quite some time ago. *Bramhasangeet* composed by him still occupies the highest echelons in the world of religious music.

O, sing aloud His name
Creation of the world-altar is His fame,
His compassion limitless,
Showers on us day and night –

This famous hymn was composed by him. They planted the seeds of patriotic songs and poetry in Bengali. It has been many years since the song composed by Gana-dada, 'Pray, how can I sing of the greatness of India, in my great shame' was sung at the Hindu Assembly. Gana-dada's untimely death occurred when I was still very young. But whoever had seen his sober and dignified, fair and well developed physique, could not ever forget him. He had great influence. It worked at the social level. He could attract all those around him and tie them together; the power of his magnetic personality prevented even a smallest bit from breaking off and detaching itself from his world.

In our country, we sometimes come across such personalities. By the sheer force of their character, they are able to establish themselves effortlessly at the centre of a family or village. If they were born in another country where big groups could form and grow in national politics, or in business and commerce, or in any universal activity, such persons would naturally lay claim to the leadership of the masses. Organising large groups and creating institutions require a stroke of genius. In our country, such skill often languishes in obscurity within large families. I think this is a terrible misuse of ability; it is akin to using a star pulled out the sky in place of a matchstick to light a small fire.

I remember his younger brother Guna-dada very well. He too filled our house to the brim. His extensive generosity encompassed family and friends, the sheltered and the obedient, guests and visitors. In his south facing veranda, or in his south garden, or on the paved banks of the pond during a fishing contest – he was a gracious presence, a figure of benevolence.

His body and spirit overflowed with a feeling for beauty and an ability to appreciate virtues in others. Various resolutions related to comic dramas and festive merriment took shelter in him and attempted to emerge in new forms and ways. Our childhood rendered us ineligible to seek entry into all of their endeavours at all times; but waves of excitement reached us from all directions and rattled our curiosities. I also remember well, a burlesque bar-dada had once written; every afternoon, rehearsals took place in Guna-dada's large visitor's hall. From the veranda of our house, we could hear uproarious laughter interspersed with a few lines from strange songs emanating through their open windows, and sometimes we caught glimpses of Akshay Majumdar Mahasay in wild dance. A few lines still linger my memory –

Don't talk to me of those things, no not again,
Why speak, what drives you to speak
Of such hilarity, oh so funny, people will freak-
Ha-ha-ha, they will laugh forever.

Whatever the big funny topic had been, I have not been able to discover to this day; but at that time, the hope that I may one day, gave me a lot of pleasure.

I am reminded of an insignificant incident where I specially experienced the love that Guna-dada had for me. I never received any awards from school except on one occasion, when I was given a book of rhymes as a prize for good character. Among the three of us, Satya was the most studious. Once, he passed his exams well and earned a prize for that. On that day, no sooner than we reached home from school, that I got off the carriage and ran indoors to break the good news to Guna-dada. He was seated in his garden. I exclaimed loudly from a distance, "Guna-dada, Satya got a prize." He laughed and pulling me close asked, "Didn't you get any?" I replied, "No I did not, but Satya did." This pleased Guna-dada immensely. That I did not win a prize myself, but was so excited about Satya having bagged one, seemed to be an admirable quality in his eyes. He openly declared this to others even in my presence. I was unaware that I had accomplished anything at all with my actions; sudden praise from

Guna-dada for what I had done, mystified me. In this manner, I was commended for not having won a prize in the first place; this was not really right. I feel that it is only proper that children should be rewarded, but not given prizes; it is healthy for children to look outwards and not inwards towards their own selves.

After lunch, Guna-dada usually came over to our building to attend to official matters of his estate. The office was an extension of their club; official duties were not greatly separated from merriment and laughter. In the office, Guna-dada sat reclined on a couch; I took the opportunity to quietly occupy a position close to him. He often spoke to me about the history of India. I was very surprised by the fact that when Clive returned home to England after establishing British supremacy in India, he was driven to commit suicide by slitting his throat with his own razor. On one hand, the foundation of a new empire was laid, but on the other, what mysterious pain lurked in the dark recesses of the human heart! It seemed incongruous that great outward success and inward failure should go hand in hand. On that day, I puzzled over the situation for a long time. On some days, from my behaviour it was clear to Guna-dada, that a notebook lay concealed in my pocket. At the slightest encouragement on his part, it emerged shamelessly from its hiding place. Needless to say, he was not a harsh critic; on the contrary, his opinion could easily have been published as advertisement. Even then, I remember some occasions very well where my childishness so exceeded my poetry that he could not stop from bursting out in uproarious laughter. I had then composed a poem on Mother India. In one stanza, I used the word *nikat-e,* or near, at the end of a line; I could not get rid of the word and nor was I able to find a suitable word to rhyme. Consequently, I was forced to use *sakat-e* or in a carriage, in the next line. While there was not even the faintest chance of the word *sakat-e* to appear there under normal circumstances, the demand of rhyming listened to no objections; as a result, without any reason, I had to arrange for a carriage to appear on the spot. Guna-dada's mirthful laughter caused the carriage with its horses to seek return by the same tortuous path that they had chosen to come at the first place and disappear forever, never to be found again.

Around that time, bar-dada sat behind a small desk on a cushion laid out on the floor of the south veranda, engaged in composing *Swapnaprayana*. Guna-dada came over to visit him every morning. His pleasure at the good things in life was as invigorating as the spring breeze towards the development of poetry. Bar-dada wrote and read aloud what he had written; his bursts of laughter reverberated through the veranda. Just as the untimely falling of mango blossoms blanket the grounds in spring, similarly numerous discarded pages from bar-dada's writing could be discovered throughout our house. His poetic imagination was so strong that he could afford to create much more than a situation demanded. Thus, he threw away his compositions in large numbers. If these could have been gathered together, a great collection of literature in Bengali would have resulted.

Though in the background, we were not deprived of the feast of poetry that engulfed our home in those days. It was spread in such large amounts all over that we had no difficulty in claiming our share. Bar-dada's pen unleashed a tidal wave of poetic imagination – the ensuing flood with the eager and tireless energy of new waves of rhythm, overwhelmed both near and distant shores. Did we understand every bit of *Swapnaprayana*? Hardly so, but as I have mentioned previously, complete comprehension of anything is not necessary to gain from it. I do not know if we could have discovered sunken treasure; even if we had, I doubt whether we would have appreciated its true value; but what we did was frolic in the waves of the sea; whatever pleasure or pain we experienced served to energise the flow of life through the channels of the body.

The more I think about those days, the more I am reminded that assemblies and gatherings, that were held then, exist no longer. As children, we beheld the setting rays of the close socialness of yester years. The intermingling of people was carried out at an intimate level and so social gatherings were a must. Special respect was reserved for the persons capable of enlivening a sitting. Nowadays people visit others on work, or to meet and exchange pleasantries, but not to enjoy a soiree. They lack time and also intimacy. Then, I observed so many visitors come and go; banter followed by laughter resounded in the verandas and in the visitor's hall.

To make an assembly come to life, to make conversation interesting – it requires a special ability that is sadly lacking today. People exist in greater numbers, but the verandas and the parlours lie vacant. In those days, all furniture, arrangements and activities were meant for many people; consequently, their splendour did not seem vainglorious. Today, the rich decorate their homes with far greater pomp and show, but it is essentially heartless and cannot reach out indiscriminately with generosity; the bare bodied, the poorly attired and the smiling faced cannot enter therein and sit down without permission. At present, all those who we copy in the design of our home and its decoration, possess their own society and abiding rules. Our problem lies in the fact that while our own social norms have broken down, there is not much scope to develop western norms; in the process most households are filled with unhappiness. These days, for the sake of some work or for nationalistic causes, we assemble in numbers of ten or more; but, to get people together for no specific purpose other than to socialise in a group is a rarity at present. There can be nothing uglier than such societal selfishness. Thus, it seems that all those people from the years gone by, who were successful in mitigating the burdens of society by their open-hearted laughter, belonged to a different nation of people.

Akshay Chandra Chaudhuri

DURING MY CHILDHOOD, I acquired a very conducive ally for my poetry discussions. Akshay Chandra Chaudhuri Mahasay was Jyoti-dada's friend and classmate. He held an M.A. in English literature. His proficiency in the subject was matched in equal measure by his love for it. On the other hand, his attraction for Bengali litterateurs like the *Baishnav* composers, Kabi-Kankan, Ramprasad, Bharatchandra, Hara Thakur, Ram Bosu, Nidhu-babu and Sridhar-kathak, knew no limits. His memory contained an immense stock of traditional songs by unknown composers. He sang these in a desperate manner, in tune, or sometimes otherwise. Objections from the audience hardly dampened his enthusiasm. He knew no restraints whatsoever, in working up the accompanying rhythm. Be it on a table, a book, or any available surface, he was adept at drumming the rhythm and engaging the audience with his performance. He was profoundly generous with his ability to generate happiness. Just as he sought whole-hearted enjoyment in everything around him, he held nothing back in paying compliments to others. As a composer of songs and poetry, his prowess was extraordinary. Strangely though, he was not in the least attached to his compositions. He hardly bothered to keep track of the scraps of paper with his pencil scribbles. His literary output was prolific but worldly indifferent. One of his poems on a woman ascetic garnered sufficient praise in the *Banga-darshan* magazine of the period. I heard his songs from many lips, the singers blissfully unaware of the composer.

The ability for uncritical enjoyment of literature is far rarer than scholarship. Akshay-babu's unbounded enthusiasm encouraged the growth of our ability to appreciate literature.

His generosity extended from literature to friendship in equal measure. On unfamiliar grounds, he was like a fish out of water; but with familiar audiences, he did not discriminate on the basis of age or level of education. He could be a child among children. On several instances, when he was leaving our house late at night after an evening of literary activities arranged by my elder brothers, I captured him and dragged him over to our study. Even here, in the dim light of an oil lamp, he had no hesitation to enliven the occasion. In this manner, I heard many a passionate explanation of English poetry from him and engaged in numerous arguments, criticisms and discussions. I read out many of my compositions in his presence and whatever little good there was, received excessive praise from him.

Music Practice

FROM EARLY CHILDHOOD, Jyoti-dada helped me the most in my education in literature and in learning to express my ideas. He was an inspiration by himself and he loved encouraging others. I engaged in unobstructed discussions on a variety of ideas and topics with him; he did not belittle me for being a mere child.

Jyoti-dada allowed me great independence; I lost my inner inhibitions in his presence. No one else dared to extend such liberties to me; perhaps he was chided by others for this. But after a spell of drought, just as the rains are essential, so also after an entire childhood of restrictions, this freedom was an absolute necessity for me. If I had not been released from my chains at that time, I might have been crippled for life. The powerful have always pointed to misuse of freedom while trying to curtail liberty, but if one has no right to misuse freedom, it is no freedom at all. The lessons, in proper use, that are derived from misuse, constitute true education. I can say with emphasis that whatever little trouble freedom has caused, it has also been responsible to direct me to the path of remedying the situation. I have not accepted anything imparted to me through excessive discipline, tyranny, being pulled by the ears and indoctrination. Until I was able to liberate myself from within, I was unable to achieve anything but pain of disappointment. Through good and bad and by overcoming all inhibitions, Jyoti-dada led me to my self-realisation; this prepared me to produce my own thorns and flowers with my own strength. From the experience, I have learnt not to fear the bad as much as the oppression of making everything good, all the time; I bow with derision to the religious and political punitive police – there is no greater harm to the world than the slavery it creates.

During this period, Jyoti-dada was busy creating new tunes on the piano. Every day, music poured out as his fingers danced over the keys. Akshay-babu and I tried to tie down the newborn tunes with our words. My lessons in song-writing commenced in this manner.

In our family, we were raised in a world of music right from childhood. My biggest advantage was that music permeated into me easily. But there was also a disadvantage. By not training adequately in music, my lessons remained incomplete. I had no right to call myself educated in music.

My Partner in Literature

AFTER RETURNING FROM my trip to the Himalayas, my freedom grew by leaps and bounds. The discipline enforced by the servants diminished; I was able to rend large holes in the school fabric and at home, I cared little for my tutors. Our earlier tutor Gyan-babu, taught me a bit from *Kumarsambhava* and a little bit of this and that rather unmindfully, before leaving to practice law. The next tutor who arrived was Braja-babu. On his first day, he asked me to translate from Goldsmith's 'The Vicar of Wakefield', which I did not mind. Thereafter, seeing the extent of tutorial arrangements, I turned myself completely inaccessible to him.

Folks at home gave up on me. No one, including myself, harboured any hope for my future. As a result, I did not expect anything and turned my full attention towards filling up my notebook of poetry. The writing was indifferent at best. My mind was filled with nothing but scalding steam – that meaningless vortex of steaming bubbles and frothing feeling was driven by my idle imagination. No beauty graced my creation, only a restless speed was apparent. It was a bubbling cauldron that seethed and boiled over. There was nothing original in the content, only my imitation of other poets; my only contribution was restiveness and a tremendous sense of regret. It is a blind revolutionary situation when there is only speed, without maturity in one's strength.

One of my sisters-in-laws, whom I addressed as *bouthakurani*, was very interested in literature. She did not read books in Bengali merely as a pastime – she enjoyed her reading with all heart. I was a participant of her literary circle.

She had special love and respect for the epic poem, *Swapnaprayana*. I too liked this poem very much. Moreover, we were nurtured in the same atmosphere in which the poem was composed and later discussed, and so its beauty easily seeped into every fibre of my heart. But this poem was beyond copying in any way. I never felt that I would ever be able to write anything like it.

Swapnaprayana is like a metaphor for a royal palace that is beyond compare. There are so many chambers, bay-windows, pictures, statues and ornamental works. There is great variety in its many halls. Surrounding the main palace, there are many gardens with hillocks, fountains, ponds and flower-beds. Not only is there a profusion of feelings, there is tremendous variation in style and composition. It is no easy task to build something so large, complete with all its components. It never dawned even in my wildest imagination that I could even attempt anything like that.

Around this time, *Aryadarshan* magazine began publishing devotional songs written by Biharilal Chakrabarty. The poetry inherent in these songs impressed *bouthakurani* by the sweetness of their composition. She memorised many portions completely. She would invite the poet to come over sometimes for dinner and she gave him a mat to sit on that she had woven herself.

Through her, I grew well acquainted with the poet. He was very affectionate towards me. I started frequenting his house at odd hours. He had a commendable heart that matched his large body. A poet's halo shrouded his mind and it was apparent wherever he went – the fine poetic being that inhabited his body was his true identity. He possessed the utter happiness of a poet. Whenever I went to visit him, I felt that happiness caress me like a soft breeze. In the afternoons, I beheld him often in the privacy of his tiny third-floor room, sprawled belly-first on the ornamental tiled floor, humming as he gently wrote – even though I was a mere child, he welcomed me with such an open heart that I overcame all traces of inhibition. Then, he would recite his poetry and sometimes sing, lost in his emotions. It was not that he was very melodious, but his singing was not out of key either – it was possible to get a sense of the tune. He sang in an emotion-choked voice with his eyes shut; whatever was his shortcoming with musical notes, he more than made up by feeling. I can still remember the songs he sang – 'A lass plays in the moonlight / pray tell me who she is, illuminated, as she dances all over my universe'. Sometimes I would put words to his tunes and sing for him.

He was captivated by the poetry of Kalidas and Balmiki. I remember that one day he recited the first *sloka* from *Kumar Sambhava* in a resounding voice and then explained that the many long syllabled 'aah' sounds in the first stanza is not coincidental – words with 'aah', starting with *deb-atma* or divine soul to *nagadhiraj* or emperor, serve to amplify the majesty of the Himalayas.

I longed to write like Bihari-babu. On particular days, I felt that I was writing something comparable – but the lady admirer of Poet Bihari at home would not let me bask in my glory. She, constantly reminded me in Sanskrit that not only was I not yet fit to acquire fame as a poet, my pace of progress towards my goal was laughable. She surely understood that if she encouraged my pride, it would be difficult to control at the end – and thus, it was not only my poetry that she criticised, she refrained from praising my singing in any way, and even compared it with the singing of others, stating that the others sounded sweeter. I too concluded that my singing truly lacked melody. Regarding my poetic prowess as well, I lost quite a bit of confidence, but since this was the only avenue of earning self-respect still open to me, I could not afford to give it up at anyone's saying – besides, I was driven by such a force that I was impossible for anyone to restrain.

Works Published

SO FAR, THE readership of whatever I had written was limited to close acquaintances. Quite suddenly, a magazine named *'Gyan-*

ankur', or 'The Germ of Knowledge', appeared. Befitting the name, the publishers also roped in a germinal poet. They commenced indiscriminate publishing of all my poetic ranting. I am afraid, that on Judgement Day, when all my good and bad deeds are tried, they would be summoned and an overenthusiastic foot soldier would march into the startled inner chambers of the publishing house, and paying no heed to entreaties of the womenfolk, drag them mercilessly to court in clear view of all populace.

My first prose composition was also published in *Gyan-ankur*. It was a piece of literary criticism. There is a bit of history behind it.

A book of poetry was published, titled *'Bhubhana-mohini-pratibha'*, or 'The genius of *Bhubhana-mohini'*. It was felt by most readers that it was the work of a lady who went by the name of *Bhubhana-mohini,* or the one who is able to awe the entire universe. Critics in several publications proclaimed a bright future for this upcoming poetess.

I have a friend from that period – he is older than me. He sometimes brought letters signed by *Bhubhana-mohini* for me to see. He was so smitten by the poetry in the book that he took to sending gifts of books and cloth to *Bhubhana-mohini*'s address.

It seemed improbable to me, judging by the feeling and language at many places, that the poems were composed by a woman. Even the letters my friend brought did not seem to have a feminine touch. But my suspicions had little effect on my friend's conviction, and his idol-worship from a distance continued.

I wrote my piece with a lot of care. I discoursed on the goals of short epic poems as well as lyrical poems with all the expertise that I could muster. My great advantage was that the printed letters are all equally indifferent and their faces give nothing away about the author, or anything about his intellectual capacity. My friend rushed in one day and announced with great excitement, "I've heard that a person with a B.A. is writing a response to your article!" The acronym 'B.A.' rendered me dumb-struck in awe. B.A. indeed! My condition now was akin to the situation I experienced when Satya called for policemen, early in my childhood. I visualised clearly that the self-proclaiming monument to short epic and lyrical poems that I had erected, was being smitten to dust by cruel blows from large quotations, and I dared not show my face to my esteemed readers. 'In what, inauspicious moment, were you born O literary criticism!' I spent day after day in anxiety. But, like the policeman from years ago, the B.A. qualified critic failed to materialise.

The Ballad of *Bhanu Singha*

I HAVE ALREADY WRITTEN that I used to read with a lot of interest, the collection of ancient poetry compiled by the joint efforts of Srijukta Akshay Chandra Sarkar and Sadacharan Mitra Mahasay. The Bengali interspersed with *Mythili* in these works was largely beyond my comprehension. However, it was for this very reason, that I applied myself to break into the realm of this poetry. Just as I was very curious towards the germ that was concealed in every seed and the treasures that lay buried deep in the earth, I harboured similar feelings for these poets of yore. By sheer perseverance, from yet to be discovered treasure troves, the hope of unearthing a gem or two of poetry kept my enthusiasm alive. Engrossed in this adventure of trying to retrieve jewels from inaccessible darkness, I was suddenly possessed by a desire to be published, covered similarly in a shroud of mystery.

Earlier, I had listened to Akshay-babu's narration of the life of the English child-poet Chatterton. I had no clue about the poetry of Chatterton; I presume Akshay-babu did not know very much either, since there is every possibility that the situation would have been far less charming if he had. However, there was a certain drama in the story that excited my imagination very much. Chatterton had written poetry forged from medieval sources that many had been unable to catch. Ultimately, the unfortunate boy-wonder committed suicide at the age of sixteen. For the time being, I set aside the needless episode about the suicide from my mind, and undertook an attempt at becoming a second Chatterton.

One afternoon, clouds covered the sky. I rejoiced in the leisure offered by the darkening cloudy day, and sprawling face down on my bed I wrote on a slate, *'Gahana kusuma kunja majhe'*, or 'Amidst a grove dense with blossoms'. The line pleased me immensely; I read it out at once to a person who could not be bothered to understand. Needless to say, he nodded seriously and remarked, "Great, it is truly very good."

One day, I accosted my friend, who I have introduced in the previous chapter, and said to him, "A worn out manuscript has been discovered in our community library. I copied the works by some ancient poet named *Bhanu Singha,* in my notebook." Having said that, I read out the poems I had recently composed. My friend grew terribly excited. He exclaimed, "I must have this manuscript! I don't think that even Vidyapati or Chandidas could not have composed anything like this. I will definitely pass on this ancient compilation of poetry to Akshay-babu to publish."

At this stage, I showed him my notebook as proof of the fact that the poems in question, could not have come from the quill of either Vidyapati or Chandidas, since these were my own creation. My friend nodded seriously and said, "No, these are definitely not bad at all."

When *Bhanu Singha* began appearing in the *Bharati* magazine, Dr. Nishikanta Chattopadhyaya Mahasay was in Germany. He had written a treatise on traditional lyrical poetry of our country, comparing the works with European literature. The respect accorded to *Bhanu Singha* therein as an ancient poet would have been impossible for a modern poet to earn. This treatise earned him his doctorate.

Whoever *Bhanu Singha* might have been, I can say with certainty that if his works fell on my hands today, I would not be fooled. It was not difficult to pass off the language as that of one of the ancient poets. The language had not been their mother tongue, it was but a literary creation; hence, there was some variation or the other in usage, in the hands of different poets. However, there is nothing untrue about their feelings. A slightly critical examination of the Ballad of *Bhanu Singha* is enough to reveal that it is a fake.

It does not have the heartfelt rhythm of our traditional music; it is merely the tinkle of a cheap organ from abroad.

Nationalism

FROM THE OUTSIDE, it was evident that there were many foreign practices that were adopted by our family, but deep inside out hearts, a nascent flame of nationalism was beginning to assert itself. The deep respect for our motherland, that lay undisturbed within my father despite many revolutions in his life, was responsible for the love of nationhood that pervaded every member of our extended family. In those days, educated people kept both their own language and nationalistic feelings at a distance from themselves. At home, my elder brothers had always kept up the practice of using our mother tongue. Once, a new relation had written to my father in English and the letter was returned unread.

With help from our family, a Hindu-fair was started. Nabagopal Mitra Mahasay was appointed as the chief organiser of the fair. It was the first attempt to appreciate *Bharatbarsha* or the nation of India as our own *swadesh* or motherland. Mej-dada composed at that time, '*Mile sabe Bharatsantan*' or 'Unite all ye children of India'. At the Hindu-fair, patriotic hymns were sung, nationalistic poetry was recited, exhibitions of traditional gymnastics and games were held and prizes were distributed among the deserving.

During the viceroyalty of Lord Curzon, I wrote an essay on the Delhi Durbar and during that of Lord Lytton, I wrote a poem – the British government of the day feared the Russians but not the writing of a fourteen-fifteen year old poet. As a result, even a copious quantity of boyish provocation in the poem failed to excite the army general or the police chief in the least. No writers to the editor of The Times had written about the indifference of the governing officials towards the temerity of a boy, and breathing heavily, displayed their deep dissatisfaction on the state of the

British rule in India. I read out the poem standing beneath a tree during the Hindu-fair. Nabin Sen Mahasay was present among the listeners. He reminded me of the incident when I was older.

At the initiative of Jyoti-dada, a meeting was convened with the venerable Rajnarayan-babu as the president. It was a *swadeshi*, or patriotic gathering. It used to be convened in a rundown building on a by-lane in Kolkata. Its proceedings were cloaked in mystery. In particular, its secrecy was its only fearsome aspect. Neither the king, nor his subjects, had any reason to be afraid of our activities. Even our relations did not have the faintest clue to what we were up to in the afternoons. Our door was closed, our room was clothed in darkness, we were initiated by hymns from the Rig Veda, we spoke in hushed tones – these were enough to thrill us to the core, not much else was needed. Even a naïf like me was a member. There was a particular madness in this assembly and our imagination took wing as we soared in its heated atmosphere. We lacked shame, fear or diffidence. In the meetings, our main preoccupation was to bask in the heat of excitement. Patriotism can be convenient at some places and inconvenient at others, but it garners deep respect within the human mind. Literatures of most countries contain volumes that seek to keep this reverence alive. Hence, however occupied a person may be, his mind cannot escape being shaken by this feeling. Through our meetings, imagination, conversations and singing, we tried to keep control of our feelings. If all roads, leading to what is progressive and what generates respect within the human mind, are closed without any gaps, there can be no doubt that it would lead to an unbearably abnormal situation. In the larger sense of governance of a country, if only a path to clerkship is kept open, a multitude of human skills are deprived the scope of developing healthily. Patriotism should be allowed avenues of expression within a state, or else humanity suffers. Lack of it, leads the hidden excitement to pulse beneath the surface – its pace is extremely uncertain, leading to inconceivable consequences. I believe that if the government had grown extremely suspicious at that stage, then the farcical bravery that was being enacted by the boys of our assembly could have resulted in terrible tragedy. The performance has long ended, not a brick has been dislodged from the ramparts of Fort William, and we laugh as we recall those days.

Jyoti-dada began displaying examples of what could be considered as dress acceptable to the entire nation. The dhoti was not suitable to be worn at the workplace while trousers were foreign, and so he attempted a compromise that not only disappointed the dhoti, it did not make trousers any happier. In fact, he took a large piece of cloth, made alternating narrow folds and tucked in one end into the waistband of the trousers, the other end cascading downward independently in a fantail that imitated the dhoti. The pith helmet was combined with the turban to create a headgear that even his most enthusiastic supporter would not have agreed to put on. To be able to don initial samples of clothing designed to be suitable for the entire populace was no easy task. Jyoti-dada climbed onto his carriage in broad daylight in such clothing with nonchalance – relations and friends, doorkeepers and coachmen stared, but it did not perturb him at all. There are many who are brave enough to risk their lives for their country, but one who, for the cause of national good, can ride a carriage through Kolkata clad in clothes designed for the general population, has to be a rare person indeed.

On Sundays, Jyoti-dada went hunting, accompanied by a large team. Most people who assembled were uninvited and unknown to us. There were carpenters, blacksmiths and all classes of people in the group. Shedding blood was of least significance in this *shikar*, or hunt and I cannot remember any incident where it had occurred. All other arrangements that made up a *shikar* were present in such abundance that we never felt the need of something as unimportant as injured and bleeding birds or animals. We set out in the morning. *Bouthakurani* or my sister-in-law, packed enormous quantities of *luchi* and curried vegetables for us to take along. Since we did not have to hunt for food, we never went hungry.

There was no shortage of large unkempt gardens in the Maniktala area. We would enter any garden in our path. Seated on the paved steps leading down to a pond, oblivious to caste and class differences among ourselves, we pounced on the food in front of us and emptied the containers in a flash.

Braja-babu was one of the most enthusiastic members of our troupe of non-violent hunters. He was the superintendent of the Metropolitan College and for some time, our tutor at home. One day, on our way back from the *shikar*, he led us into a garden and called for the caretaker and asked, "Hey, listen did uncle come by recently?" The caretaker thought he was referring to the owner and thus, prostrating himself at Braja-babu's feet, answered, "No sir, our babu did not come today." Whereupon Braja-babu ordered, "Very well, then go and pluck us some tender coconuts." Needless to say, there was no shortage of drinks to go with our lunch on that day.

We also had a middleclass landlord in our group. He was a devout Hindu. He owned a garden house on the banks of the Ganges. One day, we travelled there and had our lunch all together in a group, without observing distinctions of caste or class. In the afternoon, there was a terrible storm. We stood on the banks of the Ganges and burst out in loud singing. Rajnarayan-babu's voice lacked the ability to produce all the seven notes, but he too joined in, and just as a detailed explanation is more voluminous than the outline, so also did his enthusiastic hand waving far overtake his singing; his head swayed with the tempo and the wind tore through his long white beard. We were driven home late at night. The storm had abated and stars twinkled in the clear sky. The darkness was all encompassing, the sky was still and the village path was desolate; only the fireflies, in the dense groves of trees on the wayside, seemed to be like silent handfuls of fiery bits flung in worship.

One of the objectives of our group was to set up an indigenous factory to manufacture matches. For this purpose, members donated a tenth of their earnings. It was proving difficult to source wood for matchsticks. Everyone knows that in the right hands, sticks exercise a lot of power in our country, but what burns in that power are not matchsticks. Extensive experimentation produced a few boxes of matchsticks. These were not just valuable as products of nationalistic zeal – our expense to produce a single box of matches could have provided fuel to light the cooking fires of an entire community for a whole year. There was another slight difficulty - the matches would not light up easily, without burning flames nearby to ignite them. If only the flames of nationalistic fervour could somehow enhance their burning prowess, the matches would have survived in the market to this day.

I got the news of a young student trying to set up a cloth factory; we went to visit his works. We all lacked the ability to judge whether anything useful was being achieved, but we lagged nobody in the power to believe and to hope. Some debt had been incurred in assembling the machinery and we contributed to pay it off. At last, Braja-babu turned up at our Jorasanko residence one day with a *gamcha* towel tied around his head. He exclaimed, "Our mill produced this bit of cloth," and broke into an impromptu dance! His hair was already grey by then.

In the end, one or two enlightened people joined our group, fed us fruit from the tree of knowledge, and this bliss was broken.

In our childhood, when we were acquainted with Rajnarayan-babu, we were unable to understand him from all angles. He was a mixture of opposites. By then, his hair and beard were already entirely white, but even with the youngest member of the group he had no disaccord. Old age covered his inner youth in a white shroud and preserved its ever-freshness. Extensive erudition had not robbed him of this quality and he remained simple at heart. Right to the very end of his life, his resounding laughter knew no restraint – not the burden of age, or ill health, or the suffering all around him, or his own intellect, or the opinion of others – nothing could stem his flow of laughter. On the one hand he had dedicated his life and his whole world to God, while on the other he made endless plans, some within and some beyond his means, for the betterment of our country. He had been the favourite student of Richardson; though educated primarily in English since childhood, he was able to cast aside all obstacles of unfamiliarity and enter the world of Bengali language and literature with the fullest respect and vigour. Even though he was a very simple man at heart, his spirit was boundless. His deep love for our country was a result of his spirit. He wanted to reduce all her shortcomings, misery and insult to ashes. His eyes ablaze, his heart on fire, he would wave his arms about in enthusiasm as he sang along with us – oblivious of whether his singing was in tune or not –

In a single bond I've tied together a thousand minds,
To dedicate a thousand lives to thy service is not hard to find.

I have no doubt that this God loving, forever young, illuminated spirit that was ever sweet with laughter, whose purity and freshness were unaffected by disease and hardship, should be preserved respectfully in the treasure trove of memories of our nation.

Bharati

THIS CHAPTER OF my life was more or less a period of madness. I spent many sleepless nights, forcing myself to stay awake. Not that there was any need to stay awake, but I presume that since it was normal to sleep regularly, I was inclined to do quite the opposite. In the dim light of our lonely study I read by myself; the distant bells of a church rang out every quarter of an hour as though time was being auctioned off; from Chitpur Road leading to the cremation grounds of Nimtala, repeated cries of *'haribol'* from the processions accompanying the dead reached my ears. On countless summer nights, in the moonlight and in the strange shadows cast by row upon row of tall potted plants, I paced the third floor roof terrace like a lonesome spirit.

If you tried to pass off such behaviour as the whimsies of a poet, you would be wrong. Early in the life of Earth, there was a period governed by frequent earthquakes and bursts of fire from within. When the aging Earth of today displays such restlessness occasionally, people are surprised; however, during its juvenile years when Earth's outer shell was impermanent and the inner core hotter and more volatile, frenzied upheavals were the rule of the day. The beginning of youth is a comparable event. As long as the structure is not stable, the very ingredients that make up life are in constant revolt.

At this time, Jyoti-dada planned to bring out a publication called *'Bharati* 'or 'The Indian', with bor-dada as the editor. Thus, another object of excitement was born for us. Though I was then merely sixteen years old, I was not outside the editorial circle. By then, spurred by the audacity of youth, I had already written a sharp review of the epic poem, *Megnadbadh*. Just as the juice of an unripe mango is sour, so also is immature criticism nothing but sworn abuse. I too was searching for the best way to achieve fame by clawing at the immortal poem. I commenced my contribution to *Bharati* with this conceited piece of literary criticism.

In the first year of publication of *Bharati*, I wrote a poem titled *'Kabi-kahini'* or 'The Tale of a Poet'. This was written at an age when the writer had not seen the world beyond, but relied largely on his own unclear vision. That is why its hero is a poet. This poet does not epitomise the soul of the writer – this poet is a reflection of who the writer aspires to be and wishes to be remembered as. However, I think it is not just a matter of wish and aspiration, it is more of what the writer ought to wish for; that is to say, to be a poet at whom people would remark admiringly, yes this indeed is a poet. There is grandeur of universal love in the poem – this in itself is a fruitful device for a budding poet, since it makes poetry sound big and easy to compose. When the truth had not yet dawned in my mind and all I had was hearsay from others to rely upon, there was no possibility of simplicity and control in my composition. Then, an exaggerated effort at enhancing externally the greatness of what was truly great in itself, inevitably resulted in a deformed and laughable output. Whenever I read these compositions from my childhood, I am worried that even in my adult writing, there might exist, a profusion of such distortion and untruth brought about by excessive application. In my attempts to express anything important in a loud voice, I destroyed the peace and solemnity of the idea. I am certain that on many occasions, the loudness of my style drowned the content in print, and one day this lapse will surely be discovered.

This poetic tale made up my first book that was published. When I was at Ahmedabad with mej-dada, my second elder brother, an enthusiastic friend got the book published and surprised me by sending over a volume. I do not think he did a good thing, but the feeling that arose in me at that time was definitely not one of meting out punishment. He got his punishment however, not from the writer of the book, but from the patrons who he expected would support his endeavour. It was heard that the burden of the these volumes weighed heavy on bookstore shelves, overwhelmed up his mind and reigned undiminished for quite a while.

The age at which I started writing for *Bharati* could not have possibly produced anything worthy of publication. The evils of getting published at an early age are many – there is no method more effective in accumulating remorse to be realised during adulthood. There is an advantage however; the great fascination of seeing one's own name in print is sated at an early age. To get anxious about who read my piece, who commented and said what – a couple of printing mistakes somewhere in the text becoming a thorn in the flesh – facing such maladies associated with getting one's works published at an early age, can provide opportunities to write later on with a relatively healthy mind. The earlier, one is able to overcome the need to wave one's writing in print in front of other's noses driven by self-admiration, the better.

Nascent Bengali literature had not yet developed enough spread and influence to discipline writers with its inherent prescriptions. One had to devise this control from within while continuing to write. For this reason, it was inevitable that all sorts of rubbish were created in the interim. Unable to produce astonishing acts with the limited skills of unripe age can make the mind restless; consequently excessive stylisation and at every step, gross violations of one's natural strengths as well as truth and beauty, become evident in one's writing. To return to normal, and to have faith in one's inherent skills, happens gradually with the passage of time.

In any case, much embarrassment due to my childish literary output is enshrined in the printed pages of *Bharati*. The embarrassment cannot be attributed to mere immature writing; it is also due to arrogant impertinence, strange stylisation, and copying with great flourish.

Though I am mortified by most of my early writing, I cannot deny the value of the tremendous enthusiasm that had taken hold of my mind. It was an age to naturally make mistakes, but childhood was also a time to believe, to hope and to exult. If mistakes fuel the fire of excitement, then the flammable will be reduced to ashes; but in life, the fire would not have burnt in vain.

Ahmedabad

WHEN *BHARATI* ENTERED its second year of publication, mej-dada offered to take me to England with him. I was amazed at the voluntary generosity of the Lord of Fate, when my father granted his approval.

Prior to commencing on our journey to the foreign lands, mej-dada brought me with him to Ahmedabad where he was a judge. Mejo-bouthakuran, or my third sister-in-law, was then in England with the children, and the house was practically empty.

The judicial residence was at Shahibag. It was built as a palace for the *nawab* in the medieval ages. A thin clear stream of the Sabarmati River at the peak of summer, threaded its way through a wide sandy bed at the foot of the ramparts of the palace. Facing the river there was an enormous open terrace. Mej-dada would leave for the court. In the cavernous residence there was no other soul save for me – the only sound that could be heard was the cooing of pigeons at midday. I walked around from one empty room to the next, driven by an inexplicable curiosity. Mej-dada's books were housed on shelves cut into the wall of a spacious room. Among these was an illustrated edition of Tennyson's poems in large print. As far as I was concerned, this volume was as uncommunicative to me, as was the royal palace. My mind wandered repeatedly among its illustrations. It was not that I did not comprehend the lines at all, but on the whole, the poetry might as well have been sweet warbling to my ears. There was another book in the library which contained ancient Sanskrit poetry, compiled by Doctor Heberlein. It was impossible for me to understand the meaning of these Sanskrit poems. But the ring of the Sanskrit words and the pace of the rhymes, forced me to spend long afternoons lost in the *slokas* of *Amaru-sataka* that were as sombre as the notes from a *mridanga,* or bass drum.

I stayed in a small room in the upper level of Shahibag Palace. A hive of hornets shared the room with me. At night, I slept all by myself in that lonely room; sometimes a hornet or two fell on my bed from the ceiling, and my turning over in sleep could not have been much to their liking; for me too, it was a sharply unpleasant experience. Pacing the enormous river-side terrace late on moonlit nights was another of my preoccupations. It was during these nocturnal perambulations that I composed the earliest songs which I set to tune myself. From these songs, '*Boli o amar Gopal-bala*' or, 'Pray, let me speak O Gopala's lass', still finds a place in the collection of my poetry.

Since I was very weak in English, I spent entire days reading a variety of English books, armed with a dictionary. Right from my childhood, I was used to reading without understanding completely and not being much affected by it. Whatever little I could glean from all that I read was enough to put up a structure of the subject in my mind, and I managed well. To this day, I can still feel the good and the bad effects of this habit.

England

WE SPENT SIX months at Ahmedabad and Bombay before starting for Europe. Unfortunately, I had started sending letters about my journey to England, first to my relations and then later to *Bharati*. Now, it is beyond my powers to make them disappear. Most of these letters display nothing but the bravado of youth. It was an attempt at incendiary composition by showing disrespect, by causing hurt and by argument. A youth's mind fails to discern that the strength earned through respect, accepting others and gaining acceptance oneself, is the greatest, and that the most effective way to spread one's power is through modesty. Any expression of liking or praise was perceived as a defeat, as a weakness; and thus my endeavours to establish my superiority by antagonising others would have been laughable today, if not for the inherent arrogance and deception that are painful to me.

From childhood, I had little relationship with the world at large. At this stage, as a seventeen year old adrift in the ocean of humanity in England, there was every possibility that I would struggle to keep my head above water. But mejo-bouthakuran was staying with her children at Brighton, and in her shelter, the initial shock of arrival at England failed to make a mark on me.

Winter had already arrived. One day, as I sat beside the fireplace conversing, the boys ran in and with excitement, announced that it was snowing. I went outside in the shivering cold, and in the bright moonlight I observed the Earth blanketed with white snow. This was not the form of Earth I was used to seeing thus far – it was like a dream, nay more than a dream – and all things near pushed to a distance, it was like an unmoving, bright figured ascetic wrapped in deep meditation. Suddenly stepping out from indoors, I never beheld a more startling and magnificent beauty.

Under *bouthakurani*'s care, and driven by the pleasure of being at the middle of a variety of mischief and pestering by the children, my days passed well. The children were greatly amused by my strange English pronunciation. I had no objection to all of their games, but I could not join in wholeheartedly into this amusement of theirs. How could I explain to the children, that from a common sense perspective, it was impossible to explain why 'warm' has to be pronounced with an 'o', whereas 'worm' has an elongated 'a' sound. It was my misfortune that their mirth was directed towards me, when it was the rules of English pronunciation, which was the more deserving. I devised new means everyday to keep the minds of the two boys occupied, to make them laugh and to give them pleasure. Afterwards, numerous occasions have arisen where I had to resort to such exercising of the imagination, and that need exists even today. However, I do not feel that abundance of drive and energy any longer. It had been the first opportunity of my life to give my heart to children – perhaps that is why, the means of giving found such complete expression in a variety of ways.

However, I did not voyage from my home across the seas to enter into the comfort of another home. I was supposed to study, become a barrister and return to my country. Thus, I took admission into a public school at Brighton. Right at the start, the Principal of the school looked at my face and exclaimed, "What a splendid head you possess!" I still remember this insignificant expression for a reason; at home, the person, who persevered utmost to humble my pride had gone to extent of illustrating to me, that in comparison to many others in this world, my face and appearance could earn middle grade at the most. I hope the readers will consider it as my virtue that I believed the ruling entirely, and feeling sorry for myself at the parsimony of the Creator towards many of my faculties, I kept quiet. In this manner, observing the differences in opinion on a few issues between this person and the residents of England, I seriously thought that the ideals and reasoning of the two countries were truly dissimilar.

I was struck by one aspect of the school at Brighton – the students' behaviour towards me was not rude at all. On many occasions, they pushed in an orange, an apple or other fruit into my pocket and ran away. I believe that they behaved in this manner, since I was a foreigner in their midst.

My studies at this school did not continue for long – it was not the fault of the school. At that time, Tarak Palit Mahasay was in England. He realised that I could not achieve much in this way. He spoke to mej-dada and brought me over to London and set me up in a room by myself. The room faced Regent Park. It was at the peak of winter. Not a leaf remained on the bare trees of the park – they stood upright in rows, raising their thin uneven snow-clad branches heavenwards – observing them thus, the cold seemed to penetrate right into my bones. For the newly arrived, there is no place as heartless as London in winter. Nobody I knew lived nearby and I was not well conversant with the roads. The days of sitting alone in my room staring outdoors, returned once more into my life. But the outdoors were no longer beautiful, its brows were furrowed; the sky was a dull grey and the daylight lacked brightness like the pupils in the eyes of the dead; the surroundings seemed to collapse inwards from all directions and there was not a kind gesture left in the world. In my room there was no furniture to speak of. Strangely enough, by the grace of God, there was a harmonium. When it grew dark early in the evening, I took to playing the instrument by myself. Sometimes I had Indian visitors. I was not well acquainted with most of them. But as they took their leave, I longed to hold onto their coats and bring them back into my room.

A tutor was appointed to come and teach me Latin at home. The man was exceedingly thin, his clothes were threadbare and he seemed unable to protect himself from the cold, like the naked trees outside. I had no idea how old he was but it was evident that he had aged beyond his years. On some days, while tutoring me, he seemed unable to find the right words and he would be embarrassed. His entire family knew him to be obsessive. A certain conviction had taken hold of him. He said that at a certain time, in different places of the world, there arose a common concept; obviously, the idea was transformed based on existing disparities among civilisations, but the trend remained common. The common idea was not spread by mutual contact alone, even spatially separated areas were no exceptions. He persisted in gathering evidence to support his assertion and continued to write. On the other hand there was no food on the table at home, no proper clothes to protect from the cold, his daughters lacked the least respect for his opinion and in all probability they constantly reproached him for his obsessive ways. On some days, I could tell by looking at his face that he had found some evidence and his writing had progressed. I would then bring the subject up and try to reinforce his enthusiasm by further discussion; and again on some days, he came in very dejected, as though it was becoming impossible to shoulder the burden he had imposed upon himself. On these days my lessons would be interrupted constantly; with a vacant look in his eyes, he would be unable to concentrate in the primary Latin grammar that he was imparting to me. Whenever I beheld this man bent by the load of his obsession and the urge to write his thesis, while facing near-starvation in the process, I felt deeply pained. Even though I realised that my lessons could not progress very much in this manner, I could not bring myself to stop the tuitions. During the short while I lived at that location, I spent time feigning to learn Latin. When the time came to take leave and I sought to pay his fees, he spoke in a pitiful voice, "I just wasted your time, I didn't do my duty at all and so I cannot take any money from you." With great difficulty I convinced him to accept his fees. Despite that fact that my Latin tutor failed to present proof to support his assertion, to this day, I do not completely disbelieve what he tried to say. I still believe that there is a deep common bond among the minds of all human beings; an action somewhere causes an effect somewhere else, quite unknowing to itself.

Next, Palit Mahasay took me to the residence of a tutor named Barker. He used to prepare students for their examinations. In his house, apart from his good-natured wife, there was nothing else of beauty at all. I can understand how such tutors get students, since the students have no means to express their opinions – but it pains me to think how such a man can still attract a wife. The sole object of consolation, to Barker's wife, was her dog – but when Barker wished to discipline his wife, he punished the dog. As a result, with the support of the dog, Mrs. Barker was able to spread the extent of her pain even further.

At this juncture when *bouthakurani* called me over to Torquay in Devonshire, I ran off with great joy. I cannot express the happiness with which I spent my days there with my sweetly frolicsome child companions, amidst hills, the sea, fields of flowers and dense groves of pine. When there is admiration in both eyes, when the mind is anointed with joy and when the leisure filled day sets off on regular voyages across silent oceans to blue horizons of the mind bearing a load of untroubled happiness, why then was there no urgency in my mind to write poetry – I worried and felt hurt on several days. Thus one day, with a notebook in hand and an umbrella overhead, I went down to the beach to fulfil my duty towards poetry. I have mentioned that the place was beautiful – and it was not in the realm of poetry or imagination. A high cliff leaned eagerly into the space above the sea; in front of me, the day sky slept smilingly, rocked by the rhythmic chorus of the foam-flecked blue expanse of waves – behind me, fragrant shade from rows of pine spread out like the veil of a lazily reclining goddess of the forest. Seated on that rocky throne, I composed a poem called '*Vagnatari*', or 'The Lost Ship'. If only I had immersed the piece in the sea in front of my eyes right then, today I could think of it wistfully as having been well written. But that path is closed. Unfortunately, it is present to this day as a witness. Though presently banished from compiled volumes of my poetry, if subpoenaed, it would not prove very difficult to obtain its address.

The guard sitting watch over one's duty never relaxes completely. I got a call and again I returned to London. This time I got shelter in the household of a gentleman named Doctor Scott. I entered their house one evening with my bag and baggage. The white-haired doctor, his wife and their elder daughter were at home. The two younger daughters had fled to a relative's house, overcome by a sense of alarm at the arrival of a guest from India. I presume that when they realised I was incapable of causing any harm, they returned home.

In a short while, I became like a member of the family. Mrs. Scott loved me as though I were her son. The manner, in which the daughters too cared for me from the depths of their hearts, would be difficult to expect even from relatives.

Living with this family, I noticed something - that human nature is the same everywhere. We say, and I too believed, that devotion towards the husband enjoys a special position in our country and which is lacking in Europe. However, I did not observe any major difference between a faithful wife of our country and Mrs. Scott. Her entire mind was occupied with serving her husband. Middle-class families could not afford servants and so all work had to be done in person – thus, Mrs. Scott had to attend to her husband's small needs by herself. Before her husband came home in the evening, she would set up his armchair by the fireplace and place his fur lined slippers beside it with her own hands. What Doctor Scott liked or disliked, what behaviour to him was desirable or otherwise, his wife never forgot even for an instant. Every morning, accompanied by her only maid, she even cleaned and polished the brass work on the doors to a gleaming finish, all the way from the bedrooms upstairs to the kitchen downstairs. In addition, there were many social obligations to be met. After completing her household chores, every evening she joined wholeheartedly in our studies and music practice; to enliven and amuse the family during her leisure hours was also considered to be part of a woman's duties.

On some evenings, I teamed up with the daughters to move objects by occult power. A few of us would place our hands on a *teapoy* and cause it to move all over the room like an object possessed. Gradually it turned out that whatever we laid our palms on started to move. It was not that this was very much to Mrs. Scott's liking. Her face serious, sometimes she shook her head and said, "I do not think this is very legal." But she never forbade our childishness forcibly and continued to tolerate the unholy practice. One day when we grabbed Doctor Scott's tall hat and attempted to set it in motion by placing our palms on it, she ran in hurriedly and with anxiety in her voice said, "No, no, you cannot use his hat." Even for a moment she could not bear the thought of her husband's hat coming into contact with the devil.

In everything she did, I could discern her devotion towards her husband. When I recollect her selfless sweet modesty, I realise that the ultimate outcome of women's love is devotion. Where their love has not been blocked in any way in the course of its development, it tends towards devotional worship. Where the means of earthly pleasures abound, where enjoyment and amusement defile day and night, there this love becomes distorted; there the feminine self fails to realise complete happiness.

A few months passed here. The time for mej-dada's return to India arrived. Father wrote to say that I should also accompany them. I was gladdened by the proposal. Deep inside me, the light and the sky of my country beckoned me home. At the moment of farewell, Mrs. Scott held both my hands and with tears in her eyes said, "If you wanted leave like this, why did you have to come here at the first place, for so short a while?" This home no longer exists in London; some from the doctor's family have passed on to the world beyond while the others are lost in this world; I have no clue where they have gone, but that home is etched indelibly in my mind.

Once during winter, while walking on a street in the town of Turnbridge Wells, I beheld a man standing by the roadside; his shoes were torn in places and his bare sockless feet were visible, while his chest was not fully covered either. Since it was forbidden to beg for alms, he did not speak a word, he just glanced at my face momentarily. The money I gave him far exceeded his expectations. After I passed him and covered a little distance, he ran hurriedly from behind, caught up with me and said, "Sir, by mistake you have given me a gold coin," and having said that, he eagerly tried to return the coin to me. This event may not have stuck to my memory were it not for another very similar incident. I think it was when I reached the railway station at Torquay for the first time; a porter helped to carry my luggage from the train to the carriage. I did not find any pennies in my money bag, there was a half-crown – I handed over the coin to the porter and started off. After a little while, I found the porter running behind the carriage shouting for the coachman to stop. My initial thought was that he wanted to make further demands seeing that I was a naïve foreigner. As the carriage rolled to a stop, he said, "You gave me a half-crown, perhaps mistaking it for a penny."

I cannot say that during my stay in England no one deceived me – such instances are not something worth remembering and it would be unjust to amplify these out of context. What struck my mind is that only those who believe in themselves can have faith in others. We were completely foreign strangers who could cheat and make a run for it anytime – in spite of that, no one ever cast any suspicion on us in shops and markets.

As long as I was in England, from the beginning to the end, a farce associated itself with my life in the foreign land. I got acquainted with the widow of an erstwhile highly placed English official in India. Affectionately she called me Rubi. Following the death of her husband, an Indian friend of his had written an elegy in English in his honour. I do not wish to use too many words to describe the skill with which it was written or the power of its poetry. Unfortunately for me, it was mentioned that this poem would have to be sung to the tune of *Behag Ragini*. One day she caught hold of me and requested, "Please sing this for me in *Behag Ragini*." Quite foolishly, I decided to oblige her. There was no one else in the audience save for me, who could judge how laughable the rendering of this strange poem to the tune of *Behag* sounded on that day. The lady was very pleased to hear the lament for departed husband, sung to an Indian tune. I imagined that the episode would end there – but it did not.

I started meeting this lady quite often in invited gatherings. After dinner, when all the ladies and gentlemen assembled together, she would request me to sing that song in *Behag* tune. Everyone thought that they were going to be treated to an astonishing display of Indian music – thus they would join in to beg and request me to sing; a printed copy of the poem would emerge from the lady's pocket and my ears would turn red out of desperation. I would hang down my head in embarrassment and start singing; it soon became clear that the rendering of the elegy did not fill anyone with grief as much it did to me. At the end of my performance, amidst muted laughter, I could hear, "Thank you very much, how interesting!" Even in winter, I would be almost drenched with perspiration. That the death of this gentleman would turn out to be so traumatic for me, who could have possibly imagined at the moment of my birth or at the time of his death.

Thereafter, when I started staying at the home of Doctor Scott and studying at London University, my encounters with this woman stopped. She lived at a distance from London. She wrote quite regularly requesting me to come and visit her. Fearing the lament, I refrained at all costs. Finally, I received a telegram from her entreating me to come. When I received the telegram, I was on my way to college. Further, our return to India was imminent. I decided that before we left for India, I would honour the widow's request.

Instead of returning home from college, I went directly to the station. The weather was truly inclement on that day. Bitterly cold, it was snowing and the sky was obscured by fog. My destination lay at the end of a line and so, unworried, I took a seat in the train. I did not feel the need to inquire when I would have to get off.

I observed that the stations kept coming on the right. Thus I sat by a window on the right side and continued reading a book in the dim light of the coach. It grew dark early and I could not see anything outside. The few travellers, who had started with me from London, gradually alighted at their respective destinations.

The train left the penultimate station and ran on. Finally it stopped at a place. I looked outside and observed that it was completely dark. There were no people, no lights, no platform, nothing at all. Those who stay inside usually get no news from the outside – there is no way for travellers to know why a train stops unexpectedly at strange places – thus, I concentrated on my book once more. A little later, the train started moving in reverse – I thought, it is pointless to try to comprehend the character of the railways. But when the train came to a halt at the very station that it had left in the other direction a little while ago, it became difficult for me to stay indifferent as before. I asked a person at the station when the train would reach my destination. He replied that the train had just arrived from there. Anxiously, I asked where the train was headed. He said, for London. I realised that it was a shuttle train. Feeling disturbed, I suddenly decided to step out of the coach. I asked when I could get a northbound train. He replied, not tonight. I asked again, is there an inn nearby? He replied, not within five miles.

I had left home at ten in the morning and had not touched a drop of water since then. However, when no other path except stoicism is open, renunciation is the easiest; I buttoned my thick overcoat all the way up to my chin and sat under a lamppost at the station and continued to read. The book was Spencer's newly published 'Data of Ethics'. I consoled myself that faced with no alternatives there could be no better opportunity to read a book like this.

A little later, a porter who came by told me, there is a special train today – it will be reaching in half an hour. Having heard that, my mind filled with such excitement that it became impossible for me to concentrate on the *Data of Ethics*.

Instead of the scheduled seven in the evening, it was nine-thirty by the time I reached my destination. The mistress of the house exclaimed, "What Rubi . . . what happened to you?" It was not that I was able to give a narration of my startling journey with much pride.

The guests had already finished dinner. I thought that since my mistake was not really due to any fault of mine, the retribution would not be harsh – more so with the judge being a lady. But the widow of the high official in India said to me, "Come Rubi, come and have a cup of tea."

I did not drink tea, but on that day, thinking that it might help ward off my terrible hunger, I drank two cups of strong tea with a couple of round biscuits. I came to the parlour and saw that several ancient women had assembled there. Among them though, there was a beautiful young lady; she was an American who was engaged to be married to the mistress' brother's son; the gathering was a celebration of the successful completion of her courtship. The hostess declared, 'Alright, let the dance start.' I did not need dancing and nor were my mind and body conducive to it at that point. But people, who are exceedingly good-natured, can sometimes achieve the impossible. Thus, even though the dance was called for the young couple, and I merely had two biscuits after fasting for ten hours, I danced with women who were well past their prime.

This was not the end of my misery. My hostess asked me, "Well Rubi, where are you going to spend the night?" I was totally unprepared for this question. Dumbstruck, as I stared at her face she said, "Here, the inn closes at midnight, and so you ought to go there without any further delay." There was no lacking in courtesy – I did not have to search for the inn myself. A servant with a lantern guided me to the inn.

I thought to myself that perhaps it would turn out to be a blessing in disguise – perhaps I could find something to eat here. I asked, be it of animal origin, vegetarian, fresh or stale, could I get anything to eat. They said, drink all you can, but there is no food. I thought the Goddess of Sleep is known to be kind-hearted;

surely if she cannot provide food, she could grant me sweet oblivion for the night. But on that night, I got no place in her universe-wide equation. The stone floored room was deathly cold; an old bed and a worn out basin on a pedestal to wash one's face, were the only furniture in the room.

In the morning, the Indo-Anglican widow called me over for breakfast. In keeping with English custom, it was a cold selection. That is to say, the leftovers of the previous night's dinner were served cold. If only it had been possible to get a little bit from this last night, warm or otherwise, surely it could not have caused anyone any grievous hurt – on the contrary, my dancing would not have been as sorrowful as that of a fish out of water.

At the end of the meal, my hostess told me, "The person, for whom I called you over to sing, is ill and bedridden; you'll have to sing standing outside her bedroom door." I was made to stand at the head of the stairs. The lady of the house pointed towards a shut door and said, "She is in that room." I faced the invisible mystery and rendered the lamentation in *Behag Ragini*; what effect, it had on the ill lady, I never could glean from any verbal or newspaper report.

For the next couple of days after returning to London, I was confined to my bed, repenting my excessive and naïve good-nature. The doctor's daughters told me, "For goodness sake, do not consider this whole invitation episode as an example of hospitality of our country. It is the effect of salt from India."

Loken Palit

IN ENGLAND, WHEN I was studying English Literature at the University College, Loken Palit was my classmate and friend. He was about four years younger than me; at the age at which I am writing these memoirs, a difference of four years ought not to be discernible; but the distinction between seventeen and thirteen is so great that to bridge the gap and to establish friendship is indeed difficult. Without the experience of years, a young boy tries to keep his dignity intact. But I had no trouble of that sort at all as far as this boy was concerned; the only reason being, that I could not consider Loken to be inferior in intellect in any way.

At the University College Library, boys and girls sit down to study; it was our meeting place for informal discussions. If we had gone about our work quietly, there would have been no ground for objection – but in the plentiful steam of mirth, my friend's youthful mind was ever ready to effervesce, and at the slightest push he erupted into peals of resounding laughter. Devotion to studies has been observed to be unduly excessive among girls of all countries. Rain of silent derision, from the blue eyes of our neighbouring students at the library, remained largely unsuccessful in quelling our mirthful chatter; just thinking about those days fills me with remorse. But at that age, our conscience possessed no trace of sympathy towards those whose studies we disrupted. I never developed any headache and my mind was never troubled to face The Lord for having disturbed the peace of others at school.

It would be an exaggeration to say that we indulged merely in uninterrupted small talk and laughter within the library-temple. We also discussed literature. In these conversations, I could not consider my friend as immature in any way. Even though he had read far fewer books in Bengali than me, he more than compensated for his shortcoming, by the strength of his intellect.

Among others, one of the topics for our discussion was the formation of words in Bengali. The reason the topic came up is this. One of the daughters of Doctor Scott expressed her enthusiasm to learn Bengali from me. While teaching her the alphabet, I declared with pride, that in our language, spellings obey rules religiously, without exceptions at every step. I told her that the lack of rules for spelling in English was extremely laughable, and I would be only worried about it since we had to resort to memorising words for the purpose of examinations. But my pride did not last long. I realised that spelling in Bengali too was scarcely bound by rules; familiarity had made me overlook the fact that rules were constantly broken. Then I began searching for a rule that would explain the exceptions. I used to do this work sitting in the University College Library. I was amazed by the assistance I received from Loken in this matter.

A few years later, when Loken entered the Civil Service and returned home to India, the flow of discussion interspaced with waves of laughter that began at the University College Library, became more commendable. Loken's tremendous love for literature was like wind in the sail of my writing. In the peak of my youth, as an austere practitioner of my vocation, as I drove the chariot of prose and poetry, countless words of encouragement from Loken did not tire my enthusiasm in the least. Many memoirs and much poetry were composed in his suburban home. Our poetry and song sessions often commenced with the rise of the evening star in the sky and concluded with the end of the night, when the morning star rose and a gentle breeze blew, heralding daybreak. In the lotus garden of *Saraswati* - the Goddess of Learning, the bloom of friendship perhaps gives the greatest pleasure to the Goddess. In this garden, it was not easy to come by golden flowers, but I have no cause to complain about the fragrant honey of love.

The Broken-hearted

THE FOUNDATION OF another epic-poem was laid in England. I completed it partly during my journey home and the rest after my return. It was titled *'Bhagna-hriday'* or 'The Broken-hearted' and published, and at that time, I thought it to be well written. It is not unusual for a writer to develop such a feeling. However, even among my readers of those days, it was not very cordially received. I remember well that a little while after its publication, the minister of the now departed King Birchandramanikya of

Tripura came to visit me at Kolkata. The King had liked the poem and to wish success in the poet's literary endeavours, he had dispatched his minister just to convey this to me.

Let me paraphrase what I wrote when I was thirty about the poem I had composed at a much younger age – 'When I started writing *Bhagna-hriday*, I was eighteen years old. It was not childhood and nor was it full youth. It was at such a junction of my life from where it was not possible to see the light of truth clearly. I caught faint glimpses amidst shadows. During this period, one's imagination is lengthy and indistinct, just like shadows in the evening. The real world dissolves into fantasy. It is amusing to think that not only was I all of eighteen – it seemed as though the whole world around was merely eighteen years old. All of us lived together, not in a material world, but in an ungrounded world of fantasy. In that illusory world, intense happiness and sorrow were like emotions in a dream. That is to say, there were no true means to gauge their real measure, there was only one's own mind; thus the smallest bit grew out of proportion into one large portion'.

The period, between fifteen or sixteen years of age and twenty-two or twenty-three, was an extremely disorganised time of my life. In the geological era when the division between ocean and land was not yet well demarcated, on the early layers of mud that emerged from the water, gigantic strangely shaped amphibious beasts evolved to roam the treeless tracts. Similarly, within the dark recesses of my immature mind, emotions sprang froth uncontrollably and assuming strange forms, roamed the nameless pathless endless dark shadowy forests. Each was unknown to itself and completely unaware of its own goals. Since they did not know themselves at all, at every step they attempted to copy someone else. They tried to make up for the missing truth or untruth by an utter lack of self-restraint. In such an unobligated condition of life, when deep-rooted powers shoved against each other to emerge from within, when truth was not yet perceived as a goal that was reachable, it was then, that one tried to declare one's presence by a show of excess.

During teething in children, the buried tooth can cause a raging fever to break out in their bodies. The usefulness of this energy can only be realised when the teeth finally emerge and help to ingest food. Such is the condition also of the emotions of the mind. Until they are able to establish their own relationships with the external world, they trouble the mind like a disease does to the body.

The lesson from the experience gained in those days is mentioned in all treatises on ethics – but that does not make it any less significant. Whatever causes our desires to be concealed in us and does not allow these to emerge completely, can poison our lives. Self-interest does not permit our desires to go to their ultimate conclusion, it is unwilling to give them free rein; this is why all sorts of hurts, excesses and untruths accompany the path of selfish interest. When good deeds finally give release to these desires, then they are able to regain their normal self. The ultimate outcome of our desires is there, the path to our happiness lies there.

The immaturity of my mind that I mentioned earlier was joined by the education system and the overall outlook of those days. I cannot say for certain whether the momentum of that age has gone by now. If I look back at the age I am referring to, I am reminded of the fact that the intoxication we obtained from English literature, far exceeded the nourishment we derived from it. At that time, our Literary Gods were Shakespeare, Milton and Byron. What stirred us most in their writing was the intensity of their passion. Such passion in matters of the heart is subdued in normal behaviour of the English, but in their literature, its dominance is all the more pronounced. To inflame passions to an extreme and to drive towards a fiery end is a special characteristic of this literature. At least, it was this turbulent exuberance of passion that we came to accept as the essence of English literature. During our childhood, when our tutor who initiated us into literature, Akshay Chaudhuri Mahasay, was lost in recitation of English poetry, there was a feeling of intense intoxication. The romantic madness of Romeo and Juliet, Lear's regret at his helpless repentance, the flames of jealousy that sets Othello ablaze, in all these it is the extreme excess that gives rise to the excitement in the mind.

Our society and our small places of existence are enclosed within such dreary fences, where the tempests of the heart can barely enter - as far as possible, everything is cold and quiet; thus the pace and fury of passion in English literature struck us blows which the heart naturally prays for. It was not the happiness that arises from the beauty inherent in literature, it was the pleasure derived from encouraging revolution in a world of stability. If all the muck came up from beneath as a consequence, it was perfectly acceptable to us.

A day arrived in Europe, when the prevailing control and torment on the desires of the heart came to be done away with and as a reaction, the age of renaissance dawned; the contemporary drama written by Shakespeare is like a dance celebrating that liberation. In this literature, the debate on good-bad or beautiful-ugly was not the primary content – humans wanted to completely liberate their natural feelings entrapped within themselves and behold the ultimate face of the unbounded power it unleashed. Thus, in this literature, a profusion of very intense enlightenment and a break from the prevailing norms is evident. Strains of the great enthusiasm in this riotous display of colours in European culture entered our extremely righteous society, shook us awake from slumber and excited our senses. In a world where the heart lay subdued under scriptural rules and prescriptions without an opportunity of ever realising its true potential, we were startled out of our senses by the unbounded pleasures of a free and awakened heart that sprang forth like flames roused by notes of the classical *Dipak Ragini*.

One day, the lower octaves of English literature from the likes of Pope, transformed into the French revolution inspired high notes – the new poet of that age was Byron. The maddeningly heartfelt emotion of his poetry, reached out to the veiled heart of our straight-laced society that was so like a shy newly-wed woman, and excited it tremendously.

As a consequence, this enthusiasm manifested itself in a pronounced manner in the discussion of English literature among the educated youth of our country. Waves from that energy struck us from all directions during my childhood. Those early days were not of restraint but rather, of letting go in the excitement.

However, there existed a great difference in attitude between Europe and us. The restlessness in the European character, its propensity to revolt against being tied down by rules, migrated into its literature from its own history. There was similarity in both external and internal conditions. Thunder from the storm that raged outside permeated within. In our society, however, the true notes from whatever small wind that blew, did not cause anything more than a mere stirring of the heart – but our minds could not be satisfied with so little, and thus, in our attempts to imitate the call of the gale, we were forcedly inclined towards excess in expression. I do not feel that tendency has been overcome to this day. It will not be easy primarily because restraint has not yet arrived in English literature; everywhere there is prevalence of exaggeration and sharp expressions. That the emotions of the heart are but an ingredient of literature and not its goal, that the true goal of literature is to be replete with beauty and consequently restraint and simplicity, have not yet found recognition in English literature.

From childhood to deathbed, our minds are being influenced solely by English literature. All the ancient as well as modern European writing that have blossomed with the celebration of dignity and restraint, do not form a part of our education. As a result, I do not feel that we have been able to grasp well the method and goal of composing literature.

In those days, the person, who to us was responsible for the personification of the sharp excitement of studying English literature, was himself, a worshipper of the heart. He was inclined to believe that truth need not be perceived in its entirety, but rather, the true significance lay in experiencing truth in one's heart. He had no faith in religious knowledge and yet tears flowed from his eyes whenever he sang in praise of Goddess *Shyama*. He had no need for truth in reality; whatever excited the heart, he wished to use as truth. Rather than the need to perceive truth, his need to feel with his heart was predominant; and consequently, he had no qualms accepting whatever satisfied that need, however, small it might have been.

European literature of those days was largely under the influence of atheism. Bentham, Mill and Kant were the dominant thinkers. Our youth of the day argued over their views. In Europe, the age of Mill had evolved in history by natural progression. Driven by the human habit of cleansing the mind of all sorts of rubbish, a destructive force had arisen to break down and do away with institutions of the day. In our country, however, these were things picked up from the wayside. We did not use them in the proper manner. We used them instead as mere instigators of mutiny within our minds. Atheism was one of our fads. For this reason, we observed that there were two categories of persons in those days. One of them was quick to pick up fights and use reason as a weapon of argument in attempts to dash the belief in the existence of God in others, to smithereens. Just as shooting down birds gives pleasure to the hunter, catching a glimpse of a living creature on or below a tree makes his hands clench in anticipation of finishing it off, similarly whenever these persons spied an innocent believer unwarily sitting at ease, they grew all excited at the thought of pinning him down to the ground. For a short while we had a tutor who delighted in this sort of activity. Even though I was a mere child then, he did not spare me. Moreover, his knowledge was limited; it was not that he had searched for the truth, and after much deliberation of the available alternatives, chosen his path; he had collected the arguments from the lips of other persons. I battled him with all my might, but since I was an unequal competitor, very often I came to grief. On some days, I would be so angry that I could cry.

The other category consisted of persons who did not believe in religion, but rather enjoyed it. For this reason, like an addict, they loved to take shelter under and be thoroughly engrossed in, religious rituals and all sorts of sight, sound and smell conducive to their belief; devotion was their enjoyment. Neither of these two sides were true seekers of the truth behind agnosticism and atheism; they were driven by outbursts of emotion.

Even though this rebellion against religion troubled me, it was not that I never came under its influence. At the beginning of my youth, driven by pride in my awakening intellect, this revolt found a place in my mind too. I found no common grounds with the religious practices of our household – I did not accept them. I was only working on the bellows at a massive fire in the furnace of my heart. It was only fire worship; it was only fanning the flames with invocations; there was no other goal. Since there was no driving goal, there were no limits; the more encouragement there was, the more it leapt upwards and grew.

Just as in the case of religion, it was not necessary for truth to exist in support of the heart's passion; mere excitement was enough. I can recollect a stanza from a poet of the day –

My heart, o my heart is mine alone
Never sold it for money to anyone,
Bent and broken, however it may be,
My heart is mine and mine alone.

The heart cannot be harmed by truth, though it is inevitable that it can break or meet with other accidents; but to fall into a reverie as though it were truly broken is very essential for the exhilaration of the mind – the truth about sorrow and renunciation is not desirable, but its flavour is an object of enjoyment and thus its importance has grown in poetry. This best explains the act of excluding God and yet savouring the essence of prayer. Even today, this evil has not disappeared from our country. Consequently, where we are unable to establish religion as truth, we use thoughtfulness to enrol it in art and then give our support. In a similar manner, merely our desire to do good for the sake of our country is not true service, but it is a means to promote a feeling in the heart for the nation.

European Music

WHILE STAYING AT Brighton, I went to hear a famous soprano perform at the Music Academy. I forget her name – it might have been Madame Nilsson or Dame Albani. I had never before experienced such powerful exercising of the vocal chords. Even the expert singers of our country cannot conceal the effort of singing – they are not loath to display their difficulty in touching lower or higher octaves that do not come easily to them. The reason being, those musically inclined in our country are often satisfied recreating the song in their minds using the power of their senses; thus they tend to ignore the delicate movements of a melodious singer; to them, the coarseness outside and a certain amount of incompleteness, bring out the inner beauty of a performance. It is akin to the seeming poverty in Lord *Maheswar*'s appearance; through this, it is possible to get a glimpse of his naked magnificence. Such feeling is totally absent in Europe. Over there, external arrangements for a show have to be faultless – if there are mistakes during a performance, the singer cannot show his or her face to others. While presenting a performance, we do not think twice before taking over half an hour, to tune the accompanying instruments by twisting the knobs on the *tanpura* or banging away on the edges and rollers of the *tabla*. In Europe, such activities are limited to the backstage – what gets presented before an audience is a complete whole. Thus a singer cannot afford to display any weakness in his or her voice. In our country, offering the song is the principal goal, it is the song that we struggle to comprehend; in Europe, it is the vocalising that is more important, they attain the impossible with their vocal prowess. In our country, the natural listeners are satisfied with the song; in Europe, they pay attention to the singing. Thus at Brighton on that evening, I witnessed the strange and astounding vocalising of the singer. I felt as though circus horses were being driven through the performance. There were no obstructions whatsoever in the vocal chords, to the magic of the notes being sung. Despite all the astonishment I felt on that day, I did not like the singing at all. In particular, at several places there were imitations of birdsong, which to me were extremely laughable. In all, I kept feeling that the natural tone of human voice was being far exceeded. Thereafter, I felt more relaxed listening to male voices sing – especially the tenor voices which were unlike the gusts of ghostly lamentations that had somehow lost their way – these sounded more like voices of flesh and blood human beings. After this episode, I listened and learned to appreciate European music. However, to this day, I feel that European music and our music reside in separate chambers; they do not seem to enter the same chamber of the heart through the same door. European music is linked to normal lives of the people in a variety of ways. Thus, I can see that it is possible for European songs to be built around all sorts of incidents and descriptions and then set to tune; such attempts with tunes from our country produce strange results without any flavour for the music. Our songs seek to break free from the enclosure of everyday life; that is why there is such pathos and spiritual content, as though these were engaged in revealing the beauty of the innermost and indescribable mysteries of the world around and the human heart; that mysterious region is hidden, lonely and deep – over there exist recreational gardens for the pleasure-seeker and hermitages for the devout, but there are no facilities for the engrossed-at-work worldly being.

It does not befit me to declare that I have been able to reach the heart and soul of European music. But with whatever little authority I developed from the outside, one aspect of European music strongly attracted my heart. I felt this music to be romantic. What is really implied by romantic is difficult to explain. However, it can be said that romantic stands for the multi-coloured variety in life, for abundance, for the rhythmic dance of the waves in the sea of life, for the starting point of the conflict between light and shade over unceasing pace and rhythm; there is another aspect which is immense, which is like the unblinking vastness of the blue sky, which is like an introduction to the silent limitlessness beyond the distant horizon. In any case, my explanation may be unclear, but whenever I enjoyed European music, I have repeated to myself – this is romantic. This is the expression of the variety in human life translated into musical notes. It is not that in our music such steps have not been tried, but the attempts could not be intense or successful. The music of India gives expression to the star-studded midnight and newly aroused love; our songs cry out for the pain of separation during the world-encompassing torrential rain and express the word-stopping bewilderment born of the deep excitement caused by newly awakened spring, at the edge of an expansive forest.

Balmiki-prathibha

AT HOME THERE was a richly illustrated volume of Irish melodies by the poet Muir. I have listened several times to the spellbound recitation of these poems by Akshay-babu. The pictures entwined with the poems created a magical world of ancient Ireland in my mind. I had not yet heard the poems sung, but their music existed in my imagination. There was a harp in the pictures and it played to the tunes of these poems in my mind. I longed to listen to the Irish melodies being sung, and having learnt the notes, to sing them to Akshay-babu upon my return home. Unfortunately, in life, some desires are fulfilled and then they choose to die. In England, I listened to some of the Irish melodies and learnt them, and then the desire to complete the task of learning all the songs disappeared. Quite a few of the songs were indeed sweet, touching and simple, but the harp of the ancient assembly of Irish poets did not join in the music for me.

Upon my return home, I sang these and various other songs learnt during my stay abroad, in front of my family and friends. Everyone wondered why Rabi's voice sounded so different, quite foreign and funny. They even remarked that the tone of my speaking voice had also altered.

In the midst of these discussions on domestic and foreign music, '*Balmiki-pratibha*', or the 'Genius of Balmiki' was conceived. Most of its notes are Indian, but in this musical-drama, the music has been pulled out from its customary place of respect in an august assembly; the high flying notes are brought down to earth and put to other use. All those who have seen this musical-drama being enacted will hopefully agree that such use of music in drama has not lacked control, or has not been a failure. This is the specialty of the musical-drama, *Balmiki-pratibha*. I had been possessed by the joy of releasing music from its shackles and using it is at other places without any hesitation. Many of the songs in *Balmiki-pratibha* are broken down versions of traditional semi-classical songs, many others are set to music composed by Jyoti-dada and three are adapted from foreign tunes. The *Tillana* family of songs from among our semi-classical repertoire is easily amenable for use in drama; it has been done so at several places in this musical-drama. Among the foreign tunes, two have been used in songs of revelry by robbers in the drama and I used the sole Irish tune in the lament dedicated to the Goddess of the Forest. In the end, *Balmiki-pratibha* is not a collection of poems to be enjoyed as it is; rather it is a new experiment in music; without seeing it performed on stage, it is impossible to get a taste of its full flavour. *Balmiki-pratibha* is not what is known as an opera in Europe, it is a musical play; that is to say, music does not occupy the most important place here, merely the content of the drama is enacted to the music; sweetness of the songs by themselves, exist only at a few places.

Even before I went abroad, an occasional writers' convention used to be held at home called 'An Assembly of Notables'. For the convention, preparations were made for the reciting of poetry, singing and playing of instruments and dining. Following my return, invitations were sent out for the convention; this was its final sitting. *Balmiki-pratibha* was composed for this occasion. I played the role of Balmiki and my niece Pratibha played the role of Goddess *Saraswati*; this performance is a part of the history of this musical-drama.

Herbert Spencer has written that wherever words become diffused with even a little emotion, these can be set to music. In fact, we do not express anger, sorrow, happiness or surprise merely through words, there is music with the words. Humans developed music from the notes that accompany the exchange of words. This concept by Spencer, lingered in my mind. I wondered why, in accordance with the above principles, would it not be possible, to express our thoughts and feelings entirely set to music and presented by actors on stage. This has been attempted in the traditional art of story-telling of our country; here words sometimes shelter music, though in the strictest sense, it cannot be interpreted entirely as music. However, just as blank verse is a form of poetry, so also is this a form of music; it is not tied down by a rigorous beat, though there is a tempo; its sole objective is to clearly reveal inner feelings and not to express any pure *raga* or *tala* in its music. In *Balmiki-pratibha,* there is no great departure as far as the structure of its songs is concerned, though in the pursuit of feelings, I had to compromise with the rhythm. Since acting plays a prominent role, listeners are not affected by this shortcoming.

Following the new technique adopted for the songs of *Balmiki-pratibha*, I felt encouraged to compose another musical-drama of the same category. I named it, *'Kal-mrigaya'*, or 'The Fearsome Hunt'. It deals with the tale of the slaying of a blind sage's son by King Dasarath. This drama was enacted on a stage put up on the third floor terrace; the audience was moved by the pathos in the story. Later, I merged portions of this musical-drama into *Balmiki-pratibha*, and thus it never got published as itself.

Much later, I wrote the musical-drama named, *'Mayar khela'*, or 'The Game of Illusion', but it falls in a different category. Here the drama is not of primary importance, it is the music. Just as in *Balmiki-pratibha* and *Kal-mrigaya*, drama is the garland strung around its underlying music, in *Mayar khela*, music is the garland strung around its drama. *Mayar khela* does not depend on the pace of its storyline; it is built primarily on its emotions. That is to say, when I wrote *Mayar khela*, my mind was entirely immersed in the flavour of its music.

I never wrote anything else in the spirit in which I composed both *Balmiki-pratibha* and *Mayar khela*. A sense of excitement in the music of the period finds expression in these two compositions. For entire days, Jyoti-dada would engage in setting Hindustani classical songs to tune in the piano and churn the music with all his might. As a result, every moment brought out a beautiful facet of the *ragas* and displayed the implication of its feelings. The moment notes that follow customary slow rhythm within the ambit of their constituent rules, sped dangerously up against all conventions, the ensuing revolution brought out unimagined strengths that always stirred us deep within our souls.

The tunes seemed to speak to us clearly in a myriad of ways. On many occasions, Akshay-babu and I tried to put words to accompany the musical notes being played by Jyoti-dada. The lyrics were often not well composed enough, but they served to bear the weight of the notes.

Thus, these two plays were written in the deluge of joy that accompanied the musical revolution of breaking from tradition.

As a result, they contain rhythmic as well as arrhythmic dance and no discrimination has been made between English and Bengali content. Time and again I have bothered my Bengali readers by my views and writing techniques, but surprisingly, no one expressed disapproval over the daring attempts in the music of the two above mentioned musical-dramas, and they all returned home contented after the show. There are a few songs written by Akshay-babu in *Balmiki-pratibha* and in two of these he has used the language from a couple of places in the song ensemble by Bihari Chakrabarty Mahasay.

In both these musical-dramas, I played the main role. From my childhood, I had always been eager to act in plays. I firmly believed that I had a natural skill in this field. It is now proven that my belief was not unfounded. Prior to my first public appearance, I had played the role of Aleek-babu in a farce titled, 'I'll never do it again' written by Jyoti-dada. That was the first time I had acted on stage. Then I was very young, my voice knew no barriers and was never tired of singing; at home during that period, day after day, hour after hour, profuse and moving springs of music cascaded down, and a fine mist of musical notes spread in the colours of rainbow across my mind; the then newly arisen madness of youth rushed forward in new paths of discovery; then I wanted to test everything out, there was nothing impossible for me; I wrote, I sang, I acted and poured myself out in large measures – in this manner, I stepped into the age of twenty years. The charioteer who channelled all my energy into the turbulent excitement of the race was none other than Jyoti-dada. He was fearless. When I was a mere child, he had me saddled up for a gallop with scant attention to the fact that I was a novice and might fall down. At that young age, one day at Silaidaha, when we heard about a tiger on the prowl in the forest near the village, he took me along for the hunt; I was unarmed, and even if I had not been so, it would perhaps have been more dangerous to me than the tiger; at the outer edges of the forest, I climbed barefoot onto a frame of roughly hewed bamboo and balanced precariously behind Jyoti-dada; if the tiger attacked, I lacked even the means of insulting the beast with a few blows from my shoe. In this manner, from both inside and outside, with all sorts of danger imminent from all directions, he liberated me; he cared little for rules and regulations and he set the course for the free development of my mind.

Evensong

THE CONDITION OF my mind that I had written about earlier found expression in the volume of my poetry published by Mohit-babu under the grouping titled *'Hriday-Aranya'*, or 'Forests of the Heart'. The poem *'Punarmilan'* or 'Reconciliation' in the compilation *'Prabhat Sangeet'* or 'Morning Song', reads –

In the heart lies a deep forest;
It stretches in all directions limitless,
In its depths, I am lost clueless.
The forest is dark, its entangled growth of trees -
With a thousand arms of affection,
Rears darkness deep within.

The title, 'Forests of the Heart' was taken from this poem.

In this manner, from this period – when I had little connection with the world outside, when I was engrossed in the feelings within my own heart, when my imagination disguised in many forms roamed the realm of unreasoning emotion and directionless hope – many poems were discarded from the new collection. A few managed to find place in the volume, *'Sandhyasangeet'* or 'Evensong', under the chapter 'Forests of the Heart'.

At one time, Jyoti-dada and my other elder brothers left home to travel different places; their rooms beside the third floor terrace lay unoccupied. At that time, I took possession of the rooms and the terrace to spend my lonely days in.

Thus, when I was truly by myself, though I am not exactly sure how, the conventional norms of writing poetry that I had been confined to thus far slipped off. I think the moment my companions were no longer nearby, my soul found liberation from the reign of poetry they loved and from the forms of poetry my mind habitually conjured up in order to earn their praise.

I took to writing on a slate. Perhaps this was also a sign of my liberation. Earlier, when I wrote in an organised fashion in a notebook, there must have been a commitment to compose poems; since these were accumulating in the accounts of poetic fame, surely there was a desire to tally the sum total with that of the others, but when I wrote on a slate it was solely for its own sake. A slate seemed to reassure, 'Why fear, write whatever pleases, a mere wipe of your hand can erase it all.'

However, after writing a poem or two in this way, a burst of happiness filled my mind; my entire conscience spoke up, 'I am saved, whatever I now write is completely my own'.

Let no one take the above to be an expression of pride. On the other hand, there was conceit in my earlier compositions since pride was the ultimate reward of those efforts. I do not think that overcoming doubts about establishing oneself as a poet can be termed as vanity. Parents' initial joy over their offspring does not arise because the child is beautiful, but because the child is rightfully theirs. They may feel proud when reminded of their progeny's abilities, but that is a different matter. In the first flush of this new found freedom, I gave up all respect for the prevailing rigid rules of poetry. Just as a river does not follow a straight path as an excavated canal does, my rhymes meandered along, taking various shapes and forms. Earlier I would have counted this as an offence, but now I did not experience the slightest of doubts. As liberty seeks to spread its influence, it first breaks down the existing regulations, and then, only after it has built its own governing rules, does it give in to control.

There was only one person to whom I could read out my poetry – Akshay-babu. Suddenly confronted by these writings, he expressed delight and astonishment. With his acceptance, my path became more respectable.

Biharilal Chakrabarty Mahasay introduced a change in the meter of Bengali poetry in the poem, *'Banga-sundari'* or 'The Bengali Beauty', as in –

ak deb tarun tapan
herilen surnadir jale
aparup ak kumariratan
khela kore neel nalinidale.

Or,

One day Sun-God, the ever youthful,
Beheld in the waters of *Surnadi* an amazing sight:
A beautiful jewel of a damsel,
Playing alone among blue lotuses bright -

The new meter was not square like the earlier one, it was more rounded, and as a result it rolled along at some speed; its fast tempo was like a dance where the bells tied to the dancer's feet jangled at every step. At one time, I used this rhythm more than any other. It was not like walking on two feet, it was more akin to riding a bicycle. I got used to it readily. However, at the time I composed the poems that comprise the volume *Sandhyasangeet*, I did away with this bondage quite naturally and not out of an intention to do so. Then, I did not notice any ties at all. There was no fear in my mind. I just wrote without worrying about having to account for my actions. Due to the strength I gained by not paying heed to established traditions and writing on, I realised that what I had been searching for far and wide, was in fact available at an arm's length. Only because I had not been able to trust myself, I had failed to notice what was really mine. It was as though I awoke from a dream and discovered that the shackles around my arms had vanished. Thus I could move my arms as I pleased, and in order to express this newfound happiness I exercised my hands a lot.

In the history of my poetry, this period is the most memorable. *Sandhyasangeet* may not constitute great poetry. Its poems are sufficiently immature. Its combination of rhythm, language and feelings has not blossomed adequately. Its merit lies in the fact that suddenly one day, of my own accord, I was able to write whatever I pleased. Thus, the writing may have no particular value, but its inherent happiness is valuable.

An Essay on Singing

I HAD STARTED PREPARATIONS in England towards becoming a barrister, when my father had me called back to my own country. My failure to earn credentials disappointed some friends and well-wishers, who in turn requested my father to send me to England once again. Overpowered by his request, I set out on a journey to England for one more time. There was a relative travelling with me. However, fate struck such a blow to my aspirations of becoming a barrister, that I never made it to the English shore. For a special reason, I had to disembark at the Madras docks and make my way back to Kolkata. The incident was serious, though its cause was hardly so; people might laugh on hearing about it and I do not solely deserve their laughter; that is why, I am not describing it here. Whatever the case maybe, I started out twice to seek the blessings from *Lakshmi,* the Goddess of Wealth and was chased back on both occasions. I hope the Goddess of Law would look at me kindly for not adding to the load of the bar-library.

My father was then residing in the hills of Mussorie. I went to meet him with much trepidation. He did not express the slightest displeasure; it seemed rather that he was pleased. I am sure he felt that my return was propitious and it was God's blessing that had been the cause of such good fortune.

In the evening prior to my departure to England for the second time, I was invited to read an essay at the Medical College hall. This was my first reading of prose to an audience. The chairman of the assembly was the elderly Reverend Krishnamohan Bandopadhyay. The subject of the essay was music. Departing from instrumental music, I spoke on vocal music and tried to explain that the objective of this class of music is to bring out the meaning and significance of the lyrics with the help of the tune. The written content of my essay was relatively little. In order to win the support of my audience towards my views, I sang various types of songs in many tunes throughout the length of my talk. The chairman expressed his pleasure by comparing my singing with the sweet voice of the mythical Sage Balmiki, the composer of the epic poem *Ramayana,* and heaped much praise on me; the primary reason for this I attribute to my young age and to the fact that listening to my youthful voice, singing a wide range of songs, had moved him to tears. But the viewpoint that I had so daringly espoused on that occasion is not true, I will admit that now. The art of singing by itself has a unique nature and purpose. Where there are lyrics in a song, it is not proper for the words to seize the opportunity and supersede the music, when they are mere vehicles for the expression of the song. A song's greatness lies within itself; it should never be a slave to its lyrics. Where lyrics trail off, the song truly begins. Singing has the greatest effect where there are no discernible lyrics. What lyrics alone cannot convey, the song can. Thus, the less trouble there is from lyrics, the better. The lyrics in Hindustani classical singing are so insignificant that the tune is easily able to overcome these and present its appeal with ease. Here lies the greatness of music, where a raga in a combination of vocal notes, is able to rouse us from deep within. However in Bengal, since many years, the supremacy of lyrics has been such that pure vocal music has never been able to gain a foothold. It has had to survive under the shelter of its elder sister – poetry in song. Subjugated to the control of all types of singing ranging from the *padabali* repertoire of the *Vaishnava* poets to the *tappa* of Nidhu-babu, it has tried to spread its sweetness all around. However, in this country, just as a wife is able to rule over her husband only after accepting his dominance, so also does song get ahead after accepting the burden of following its lyrics initially. This has been experienced time and again while composing songs. As I hummed and wrote a line, 'Do not keep your secret my love, concealed in your mind', I felt the tune blow the words to heights that would have been unachievable to the lyrics, if they chose to walk alone. Then I felt that the secret I was pining to hear had dissipated among the dark green of the trees of the forest, it lay submerged in the silent brilliance of moonbeams, it lay concealed beyond the distant blue horizon; it was the most profound secret of the ocean, land and sky. Very early in my childhood, I heard a song that went, 'Who dressed you like a stranger, my lady!' That one line created such a wonderful picture in my mind that even today, the words ring in my ear. One day, I too succumbed to the charm of the line and sat down to compose a song. Humming the notes aloud, I wrote, 'I know, yes I know you my lady, o stranger of mine' – if the tune was not present to hold the words aloft, I cannot say whether there would have been any feeling in the song. It was due to the effect of the tune that a beautiful image was conjured in my mind. My mind wandered afar seeking the stranger who travels across our world, and the mysterious river on the banks of which stands her home; certainly, she is the one whose glimpse I catch time and again on crisp autumn mornings and during sweet summer nights, the one whose touch I sometimes feel in the depths of my heart, the one whose voice I hear at other times as I press my ear to the sky. The tune dragged me over the doors of the greatest enchantress of the entire universe, who was also a stranger, and I wrote –

> I roamed the universe and then
> I've come to see you again,
> I am a guest at your doorstep, o stranger o' mine.

Many years later, I heard someone singing on the streets of Bolpur–

> How does the ancient bird find a way to fly in and out
> of the cage?
> If only I could reach out, and shackle it in place.

I observed that the *baul*'s song had the same yearning. Sometimes the ancient bird enters the cage to speak of the strange life beyond its fetters; the mind wishes to imprison it in the cage, but in vain. How can we speak of the silent coming and going of this ancient bird save through the tune of a song!

I always hesitate before publishing a volume of songs. The reason is that the essence of the songs goes missing. Holding on to the constituent parts that make up vocal music without the music as a whole, is like restraining the rat which is the symbolic vehicle of Lord *Ganesha,* while letting the God go his way.

On the Shores of the Ganges

WHEN I RETURNED from the abortive attempt of journeying to England for a second time, Jyoti-dada was residing in a bungalow located in a garden beside the Ganges at Chandannagar; I accepted his offer to stay there. It was the same Ganges I remembered so well! Once again, that indescribable languid happiness and yet, with a lingering sense of sorrow and anxiety, filled the days and nights spent listening to the poignant gurgle of the dark smoothly flowing river. This was my place on Earth; this was where I was constantly nourished by my mother's own hands. To me, the complete surrender of my body and soul to this light that filled the heavens of Bengal, this southern breeze, this flowing Ganges, this royal languor, this blue of the sky and this lofty space amidst the greenery of Earth that stretched to all horizons – was as essential as water for thirst and food for hunger. It was not very long ago, but a lot has changed since then. Our hidden abodes beside the Ganges under the abundant shade of trees have been invaded by factories; like so many serpents with hoods raised to strike, they hiss noisily as they exhale their sooty dark breaths into the atmosphere. Nowadays, within our minds, even during the heat of midday, the extent of the relaxing charm of Bengal has narrowed considerably. Everywhere in our country, a sense of a busyness lacking leisure, has spread its vicious tentacles. This maybe good in a way, but whether it will be good in the long run, I cannot say for certain.

Those beautiful days spent on the shores of the Ganges floated by one after another like lotuses in full bloom, cast into the current as offerings to the Gods. Sometimes on dark rainy days, I would set one of Vidyapati's poems to several variations of notes based on the monsoon ragas, and while playing on a harmonium, sing away rain-lashed flood engulfed afternoons; at some other time we would set off on a boat during sunset, Jyoti-dada played on the violin while I sang aloud; starting with *Raga Purabi*, when I finally reached *Behaag*, the store of golden toys on the western sky would have completely sold out its wares as the moon rose over the eastern horizon. When we finally returned to the garden shore, placed cushions on the floor of the riverfront terrace of the bungalow and sat down, land and water were overcome by bright stillness and peace, there were no boats on the river, the line of forest along the shore was clad in dense darkness, the unruffled smoothness of the river surface twinkled with reflections of distant light.

The estate we were living in was famous as Moran Sahib's Garden. From the *ghat* on the Ganges, a flight of stairs led to a massive stone paved veranda. This was at the entrance to the bungalow. All the rooms were not at the same level – some were built higher while some others were a few steps lower. The rooms were not aligned either. There were stained glass panes on the windows of the front hall situated above the *ghat*. One of the panes depicted a scene of a swing tied to a branch of a tree in a dense grove, a couple sat swinging in the light and shade of their hidden bower; another showed stairs leading to a castle where brightly dressed men and women could be seen, some climbing up while others climbed down. As sunlight fell on the glass, the pictures filled with light. From a faraway land, a festival in the distant past spread its fable soundlessly in the light, while the sweet romance of the couple on the swing lost in their own world in a sunny clearing, caused the pain of their unknown tale to diffuse into the forest surrounding us. On the uppermost story, there was a round room open to all directions. I selected that place to write my poetry. Sitting there, all I could glimpse were the sky and the crowns of the trees. I was composing the poetry of '*Sandhyasangeet*' or 'Evensong' during this period; the following lines were directed to this room –

Clasped to the bosom of the sky
Amidst spreading clouds in view,
It's here that that I've set up my home
To, dedicate this poem to you.

From this period onwards, there rose a reaction among poetry critics that I was a poet who wrote in broken meter, using juvenile language. Everything I wrote was obscured by smoke and was shadowy. However unpleasant their words sounded to me then, their views were not unfounded. Truly, my poetry possessed nothing of the harshness of the reality of life. During childhood, from the way I grew up far from contact with humanity as I was imprisoned at home, how could I acquire the resources to write about the world outside? However, I cannot accept one criticism. When they declared my poetry to be hazy and unclear, they also added directly or otherwise that it was the fashion of the day. Those with very good eyesight often grew angry, when they came across a youth sporting glasses, thinking that the glasses were being used merely as an ornament. The ill-repute associated with a poor fellow possessing weak eyes was acceptable, but to pretend to do so was definitely too much.

Just as a nebula cannot be considered to be beyond creation since it is an evolutionary stage in the formation of the universe, similarly to dismiss the unrevealed in poetry as lack of application on the part of the poet, would be a denial of truth in the art of composing poetry. Based on the situation, humans are sometimes struck by a feeling which reflects the pain of the indescribable and the anxiety of an indistinct emotion. Since this is a universal truth, how can we call its expression untrue? It would not be right to say that such poetry has no value, though arguments may rage on the subject. But on the other hand, would it not be an exaggeration to consider that it possesses no value at all? Humans try to speak out their heart through the medium of poetry; if a poem talks about any condition of that heart, it becomes a cherished piece; and if it does not, then it is cast away and forgotten. Thus, there is no sin in expressing the unsaid prayer within the heart; on the contrary, it is a crime not to do so. There is a dichotomy within the human mind. Concealed deep behind all outer incidents, all worries and emotions associated with external life, there exists a being, whom we do not know very well and often tend to forget, but we cannot wipe out his existence altogether. When the external world is not in tune with its corresponding inner being, when the understanding between the two is not beautiful and complete, then the resulting deep seated pain keeps hurting humanity. I cannot give any special name to this pain, it defies description, and thus the language of its cry is not clearly decipherable; rather than meaningful words, it contains more meaningless notes. The truth at the bottom of the sorrow and pain, sought to be expressed in *Sandhyasangeet*, lies deep within that inner mystery. My life was being thwarted from reaching a place where all lives were united into one. Just as the consciousness that is lost during sleep tries to battle nightmare and somehow return to an awakened state, so also the inner being tries to overcome all external complications and rescue itself; instances of that fight from the deepest and invisible realms within us have been expressed inexplicitly in *Sandhyasangeet*. In every creation, there is competition between two forces, and so also in poetry. Where, the disaccord is too large, or where the understanding is complete, perhaps no poetry can be written. But where the pain of disagreement is trying to reach out for understanding and to express itself, poetry bursts out like notes of a raga from the entrapped breath within a flute.

After the birth of *Sandhyasangeet*, though conches were not blown from the household of the new-born, it was not as though there were none to accept it with love and respect. I have already mentioned this incident in an essay elsewhere – Ramesh Datta Mahasay's eldest daughter was getting married and Bankim-babu had just turned up at the gate of the wedding hall; Ramesh-babu was about to welcome him with a garland when I arrived there. Bankim-babu quickly transferred the garland to my neck and said, "He truly deserves this garland. Ramesh, have you read *Sandhyasangeet?*" Ramesh-babu replied, "No". The opinion, that Bankim-babu went on to express about one particular poem from the collection, was my greatest reward.

Priya-babu

BY COMPOSING *SANDHYASANGEET*, I earned a friend whose encouragement shone favourably on my attempts at developing my poetry further. He was Srijukta Priyanath Sen. Earlier, after reading *Bhagna-hriday* he had given up on me, but with *Sandhyasangeet* I won him over. All those acquainted with him know well that he is a sailor on the seven seas of literature. He frequented every street and alley of both domestic and foreign literatures of many languages. Seated beside him, it was possible to gaze all at once into the many distant horizons of the world of feelings. This proved very useful to me. He could discuss literature fearlessly; his likes and dislikes were not about his personal taste. On one hand, it provided entry into the treasure house of world literature, while on the other it reinforced confidence and belief in my own ability – both these aspects of his friendship, early in my youth, proved useful in more ways than I could enumerate. In those days, I made him listen to all the poems I wrote, and through his happiness the poems were ceremonially inducted into the collection. If I had not got that opportunity, then rains would not have nourished the seedlings planted at an early age, and how the crop would have fared is difficult to assess.

Morning Song

SITTING ON THE shores of the Ganges, apart from the poetry in *Sandhyasangeet*, I also wrote some prose. The topics were not limited to any fixed subject; these were also, in a way, what I wrote as it pleased me. Just as young boys hold on to the strings of their kites quite carelessly, this too was akin to that. When spring arrives within the mind, little bits of colourful impressions float around, and in these days of leisure, I was struck by a fancy to capture and collect these bits. The truth was that I was being driven along by an obsession; my mind swelled with pride and declared that I will write whatever I wished – I had no idea about the content, but the thought that I alone will write was the source of the excitement. The little prose pieces were published at one time under the title of '*Bibidha Prasanga*', or 'Miscellaneous Topics'; these were buried along with the first edition, with no scope of a new lease of life in a second.

I think it was around this time that I started on a long historical novel titled '*Bouthakuranir Hat*', or 'The Fair of the Sister-in-law'.

In this manner, after some days were spent on the banks of the Ganges, Jyoti-dada moved to a house located at 10 Sudder Street, near the museum at Chowringhee in Kolkata. I went with him. Over here too, I continued gradually on the novel and was also progressing poem by poem on the *Sandhyasangeet* collection, when suddenly there was an upheaval within my mind.

One late-afternoon, I was pacing on the roof terrace of our house at Jorasanko. The glow from the setting sun commingled with the pale light at the end of day, made the onset of the evening especially captivating to my mind. Even the walls of the adjacent buildings seemed beautiful to me. I wondered whether this lifting of the veil of banality from the everyday world was merely a trick of the falling darkness. But it was definitely not so. I saw clearly that evening had fallen inside me, I was enveloped by it. When I had been harshly illuminated in daylight, whatever I saw or heard, I collected and stowed away by myself. Now, since I moved away, I was able to perceive the world in its natural form. This form was not insignificant – it was full of joy, it was beautiful. Thereafter, sometimes I tried to see the world as an observer after willingly moving away from situations, and this brought much joy to my mind. I can remember one day when I tried to explain to a relative at home, how to observe the world properly while lightening one's burden on it at the same time – I had no success at all. After that, I had an experience that I cannot forget.

Looking out from our residence beyond Sudder Street, I believe it was possible to see the trees of the Free School garden. One morning I stood on the veranda gazing in that direction. The sun was rising from behind the foliage. Suddenly, a veil seemed to lift away from my eyes. I saw the entire world enveloped in an amazing divine glory, waves of happiness and beauty rolled onto every shore. In an instant, the light of the world penetrated the layers of sorrow in my heart and dispersed everywhere within me. On that very day, the poem *'Nirjhar-er Swapnabhanga'*, or 'The Awakening of the Cascade' burst forth and flowed out like a waterfall. I finished writing, but the curtain did not fall upon the joyousness of the world. I disliked no one or nothing any longer. On that day or may be the next, there was an incident that surprised me. There was a man who sometimes used to ask me questions of the type, "Well *mosai*, have you ever seen God with your own eyes?" I had to acknowledge that I had not; he would then reply, "I have." If I then asked, "What did you see?" He would reply that God filled up his vision completely. Such spiritual discussions with others cannot be pleasant at all times, more so when I was overcome by the urge to write. However, since the man was harmless, I could not bring myself to restrict him, and so I tolerated it all.

This time, when this man came at noon, I greeted him with joy and exclaimed, "Come, come." It was as though the veneer of a dull and strange person had peeled off him. The person whom I welcomed with such happiness was his inner being – I had no differences with him, in its place there was a relationship. When I felt not at all troubled and was not worried about my time being wasted, I was intensely pleased – it seemed that the web of falsehood around me had disappeared; in this connection, all the pain I had directed repeatedly towards myself for so long was proven baseless and unnecessary.

I stood on the veranda and was amazed at the gait, the physique and the face of every passerby on the street, whether it was a labourer, a worker, or anyone else; everyone seemed to flow on like divine waves on the world-wide ocean. Since childhood, I had grown used to seeing with my eyes, now I began to perceive with my entire consciousness. When two youths went past, filled to the brim with untroubled laughter, with one's arm across the other's shoulder, I could no longer accept the incident as mere happenstance – I seemed to perceive the unending pleasure, rise from the unfathomable depths of the world ocean, and cause laughter to break out everywhere.

Never before had I noticed the varying speeds at which the different parts of the human body moved while engaging in small ordinary tasks; now, at each and every moment, the music in the motion of the entire human body amazed me. I did not see each action to be separate from the other, but as a collective whole. At this very moment, in different communities worldwide, millions of people are active in countless activities driven by many needs – thinking about the energy of the whole body of mankind spread over the entire earth, I could perceive a hint of a most beautiful and unified dance. Friends laughing with each other, mothers nursing their children, a cow licking the body of its neighbour, the unending timelessness in all these scenes hurt my mind with blows of amazement. During this period, I wrote –

My heart opens its doors with welcoming grace,
The world enters in loving embrace.

This is not an exaggeration of my imagination. Indeed, I did not possess the faculty to express what I had experienced.

For a certain period, I lost myself in such a state of utter joy. Suddenly, Jyoti-dada and his family decided to go to Darjeeling. I thought this to be a good move for me – perhaps I could realise better and deeper, amidst lofty mountain peaks, what I had observed in crowded Sudder Street. At least, I could come to know how the Himalayas would express themselves from this perspective.

I roamed tracts of *Debdaru* forests, I sat beside springs, I bathed in their waters, I started at the cloudless vistas of snow-clad peaks – but I did not find what I had thought would be easy to do so. There were merest hints, but no resulting vision. I had been gazing at a gemstone, but now that ended and I found myself looking at its box instead. However embellished the box might have been, there no longer was any apprehension of mistaking it to be empty.

The songs of *'Prabhatsangeet'* or 'Morning Song' stopped playing in my mind, but as its distant reverberation, I wrote a poem titled *'Pratidhwani'* or, 'The Echo' at Darjeeling. This poem turned out to be so incomprehensible, that two friends once placed a bet to see who could arrive at a better interpretation. Disappointed, one of them approached me in secrecy to get a better comprehension of the poem. I do not think he was able to win his bet with my help. The only happy part of this episode was that none of them had to face defeat and part with their money. Alas, how distant were the days of clarity when I wrote about the lotus or the rain-filled lake!

No one writes poetry to explain something. Feelings of the heart try to gain a form through poetry. Consequently, when someone says 'didn't understand' after listening to a poem, it is a difficult situation for the poet. If someone sniffs a flower and says 'didn't understand at all' he must be reminded that there is nothing to understand, it is only a fragrance. He might retort, 'that I know, but why fragrance, what does it mean?' He must either be stopped from continuing further, or he has to be told sharply, that the inner joy of nature finds expression as floral fragrance. But the difficulty in this case is that the words used to write poetry have meaning. Hence, by using a rhyming structure and other means, the usual ways of using words are turned upside down by the poet, who then devises various means to express his feelings while suppressing the true meanings of the words. Feelings are not knowledge, not science, not useful in any way and like tears in the eyes and a smile on the face, they are merely inner reflections. If you can, mix spiritual knowledge, science or other subjects requiring intelligence with it, but that is secondary. While crossing a river in a small ferry, if you are able to catch fish, it is to your credit; but then the ferry is certainly not a fishing vessel; cursing the boatman of the ferry for your not being able to lure fish is gross injustice.

I wrote the poem *Pratidhwani* many years ago; presently, it does not catch anyone's eye. Hence I do not have to respond to questions about it from anyone. Good or bad, however it may be, I can say this with emphasis that I did not write this poem to confuse the readers on purpose, and I did not attempt to convey any serious spiritual message by concealing it in the lines of poetry.

The truth is that an extreme anxiety had germinated in my mind and it was seeking a path to express itself. Unable to name the target of the anxiety in any other way, I called the being my 'Echo' and wrote,

O Echo,
I suppose I love you,
I suppose it is you and no one else.

A few notes are born at the very centre of the universe – its sound emerges from the voice of the loved one, bounces off from all objects of beauty in the world, and the resulting echo enters our heart. I suppose we love the echo more than any object, since we are able to experience it; we had not directed our senses towards this perception and yet one day, this feeling overwhelms our entire consciousness.

So far I had been looking at the world from the outside, and hence I had been unable to perceive it as a joyous whole. Suddenly one day, a spark emerged from the very centre of my inner being and spread across the entire universe, and in the resulting light, I perceived the world, not broken down to specific incidents or specific objects, but in its entirety from the very beginning to the end. Thus a feeling grew in my mind, that from the deepest and innermost recesses within us, strings of notes arise and spread across time and space – after impinging on all objects at every age everywhere, the echo stream returns to its source, borne on waves of joy. The echoes of the notes, at the moment of re-entry into their limitless source, perplex our minds with their inherent beauty. When notes from a musical genius overflow from his heart, he experiences an intense joy; but when the tune finds its way back to his heart, the joy doubles. When the song of the Universal Poet exultantly returns to its source and we let it stream over our consciousness, we are able to glimpse the indescribable beauty of the ultimate form of the world. Where there is this realisation lie our joy and attachment; there, faced with the limitless, our minds are set free to float in the torrent of joyful bliss. This is the significance of this yearning for the universal beauty. The song that emerges from the limitless and approaches humanly limits is true, it is beneficent, it obeys rules and it has a definite form; its echo that returns from the limiting to the limitless is beauty, it is happiness. It is impossible to touch or to hold on to, and that is why its pursuit causes one to run away from home. In the poem *Pratidhwani*, through song and metaphor, I have attempted to express this realisation of mine. I cannot hope that the result is clear, since the attempt itself was not very cognisant of its own goal.

When I was somewhat older, I wrote a letter on *Prabhatsangeet*; let me present an excerpt here –

> 'There's none in this world who is not within my soul' – this describes a special condition of a particular age. When the heart awakens at first, it extends both arms forward and yearns for the entire world – just like a child with newly emerged teeth, who feels that he can stuff everything within reach into his mouth.
>
> Gradually, it is possible to understand what the mind really wants and what it does not. Then the expanding steam within the heart seeks out a narrow path to inflame the yearning. If we demand the entire world, we would come up empty handed; but it we are able to concentrate on something with our complete body and soul, it is possible to find the gate leading to the limitless. *Prabhatsangeet* is an expression of the initial passionate outburst of my innermost feelings, captured without discrimination.

The joy of the initial passionate outburst that is diffused everywhere, drives us towards a special realisation – as it fills out, a lake desires to flow out in a stream – at that stage, the infatuation of courtship results in deep and mature love. In fact, in a way, love seeks a narrower path than infatuation. It does not try to devour everything in one bite but tries to taste a bit at a time. Only then, with single-minded devotion, love is able to experience the whole in a part, the limitless within limits. Then the consciousness, through the realm of the perceptible, expands into the imperceptible infinite. And the ensuing result is not limited to an undefined happiness within the mind – along with the external world and whatever is perceptible, the feelings of the heart are transformed into universal truth.

In the compilation brought out by Mohit-babu, the poems of *Prabhatsangeet* have been grouped under a chapter titled 'Emergence'. This is because the poems are a proclamation of the emergence of the self, from the depths of the heart, to the world outside. Thereafter the heart, as a traveller in the path of happiness, sorrow, light and darkness – singly, in parts, in many tunes and rhythms and in diverse other ways - unites with the world. Finally, the stream of realisation will flow past many paved *ghats* along its banks, until one day it reaches the limitless expanse once again, but that vastness is not one of indefinite extent, it is the infinity of complete truth.

During my childhood, I developed an easy and close relationship with the world of nature. Every coconut palm in our garden appeared to me in their true state. On returning from Normal School at four o'clock in the afternoon, I observed thick bright clouds amassed in the blue sky behind our terrace – my mind rejoiced with deep pleasure at the sight, and I have never been able to forget that moment. No sooner than I woke up in the morning, the jubilation of the world beckoned me outdoors as a playmate; at noon, the depth of the entire sky and the hour grown intense with heat made me renounce the world; and the darkness of the night opened the secret door to a mysterious path to the realm beyond the extent of what was possible, or impossible, to the fairytale kingdom across seven seas and thirteen rivers. After that, aroused by early youth, when the heart began to make its own demands, the easy relationship that existed with the world outside suffered. In this way, driven by the craving of the weak heart, the balance between the internal and external worlds broke apart and I lost the easy control I had possessed for so long; *Sandhyasangeet* speaks of this pain. Finally, the shut door was suddenly dashed open, I know not with what blow, and my lost world came back to me. Not just returned, but through the intervening distance of separation, I experienced it in its entirety. What is easily obtained, when earned through difficulty, generates greater satisfaction. Thus, when I got back the world of my childhood through *Prabhatsangeet,* it was a greater discovery. In this manner, through easy awakening, separation and reunification with nature, the first act of my life was concluded. It would be untrue to say that it was over. The next act of the play, starting once more in a more diverse manner and through more contentious issues, reached out for a greater goal. Every human comes to this world to fulfil a unique role in a play – from act to act, his circle of influence grows larger to encompass a greater extent of the world; in different scenes it may be mistaken to be different worlds, but in the end, it can be seen that the centre of the circle is one and the same.

When I was writing *Sandhyasangeet,* pieces of my prose were being published under the title 'Miscellaneous Topics'. From the period I was writing *Prabhatsangeet,* or may be a little later, such pieces were compiled and published as 'Discussions'. From the difference in the style and content of the two volumes, it is not difficult to gauge the author's state of mind.

Rajendralal Mitra

AROUND THIS TIME, a germ of an idea about setting up an association of Bengali litterateurs took root in Jyoti-dada's mind.

The aim of this assembly was to firm up technical terminology in Bengali, and in general, to promote Bengali literature in every possible way. There were almost no differences between the objectives with which modern literary associations were conceived of, and our planned association.

Rajendralal Mitra Mahasay accepted the proposal with enthusiasm. He was nominated to be the president of the association. When I approached Vidyasagar Mahasay to join the association, after listening to the objectives and the list of committed members, he said, "Let me give you an advice, give up people like us – you cannot achieve much with 'stalwarts', since no one would agree with each other." And having said so, he refused to join the association. Bankim-*babu* became a member, but I cannot say that he was available for committee work.

In fact, all work related to the association, during the few days it survived, was handled by Rajendralal Mitra. The first task we took up was to fix geographical terminology. The entire first draft of the list was corrected by Rajendralal. It was published and distributed among all the other members for discussion. We resolved to list all the countries of the world in accordance with the prevalent phonetic pronunciation in each country.

Vidyasagar's words proved to be true – it was impossible to get any work out of the assembled group of stalwarts. The association withered just after it had taken root.

However, Rajendralal Mitra was ambidextrous. He was an association by himself. I was fortunate to get his acquaintance on this pretext.

So far, I have come to know many great literary personalities, but the brightness with which the memory of Rajendralal resides in my mind is unsurpassed.

Near Manicktala Garden, where the Court of Wards was situated, I went to meet him whenever I wished. I would go in the morning and observe him busy in his studies. Due to the indiscretion of youth, I disturbed him at work without hesitation. But I never felt his displeasure even for a moment. As soon as he saw me, he would put his work aside and start talking. Everyone knew that he was hard of hearing. For this reason, he rarely gave me an opportunity to ask questions. He would pick a topic and carry on himself. I went to him, just to hear him speak. With no one else did I find as much scope to reflect on so many new subjects. I listened to his discourse spellbound. I believe he was one of the main members in the committee that selected textbooks in those days. He read all the books sent to him, making notes on the pages with a pencil as he went along. On certain days, he would pick some book he was engaged with and speak on language usage and linguistics, which benefitted me greatly. There were few subjects he did not discuss well and whatever topic he picked, he was able to describe it with lucidity. Without disrespect to the other members of the association, if it had been possible to get Mitra Mahasay alone to do all the work, there is no doubt that he could have contributed singularly to the growth of our literary association.

Rajendralal Mitra was a thoughtful writer, but this alone was not the main reason for his glory. His humanity shone in his very being. With no disregard for one as ignorant I was, he discoursed philosophically on weighty matters – though there hardly existed anyone else his equal in vigour. I was even able to extract from him an article titled '*Yama's* Dog' and to get it published in the *Bharati*; there is no other famous writer of that period, whom I dared to pester as much, and hope for indulgence. However, dressed for battle, his was a fearsome appearance. In the municipal assembly and in the senate, his opposition used to be afraid of him. In those days, Krishnadas Pal was wily while Rajendralal was the valiant one. He was never dependent on anyone for support, in his rivalries with famed warriors and he did not know defeat. In the Asiatic Society, he hired several Sanskrit scholars to write books for publication and for discussions on antiquities. I can recollect that many, from among the malicious and the jealous, declared that while the scholars did all the work, Mitra-mosai slyly grabbed and enjoyed the fame resulting from their efforts. Even today, it is sometimes possible to observe situations where the person who is a mere machine gradually begins to think, 'I am successful and the driver of the machinery is but an unnecessary decoration'. If the pen possessed consciousness, one day while writing, it would have surely thought, 'I do all the writing, but while my mouth bleeds ink, the writer's fame grows brighter'.

Upon his death, this unequalled lion-hearted personality of Bengal never received any special respect from his fellow countrymen. One reason for this was that Vidyasagar's death immediately followed his, and the ensuing outpouring of grief was effective in covering up the pain of his loss from the consciousness of the people. There is another reason – he did not have that many literary achievements in Bengali, and as a result, he did not get an opportunity to establish himself in the hearts of the common people.

Karwar

NEXT, FOR A WHILE, we the residents of Sudder Street took shelter in the distant seashore town of Karwar.

Karwar is the principal town of the Carnatic region in the southern part of Bombay Presidency. It is the birthplace of cardamom and sandalwood, situated on the Western Ghats of the Malabar Coast. Mej-dada was posted there as a judge.

This tiny seaport hemmed in by mountains was so secluded, so hidden, that urbanisation had not been able to take on its true form. A half-moon shaped sandy bay seemed to extend its arms into the blue expanse of the sea as the physical expression of a yearning to capture the infinite in a close embrace. At the edge of a wide beach there was a thick Casuarina forest; at one end of the forest, a tiny river called Kalanadi flowed out to the sea through a narrow gap between its companion mountains. I remember, one evening, during the waxing phase of the moon, we set out on Kalanadi in a small boat, travelling upstream with the tide. We went ashore at one spot to take a closer look at an ancient fortress built by *Shivaji,* before setting off once again.

On the silent forest, on mountains and on the swiftly flowing current of the narrow river, the moonlit night in meditation seemed to cast a spell with magical lunar hymns. We came ashore and proceeded to the fenced enclosure of a farmer's hut that had been swabbed clean with cow-dung. We dined sitting on mats placed on the floor of the enclosure, bathed in moonlight that crept over the slanted shadows cast by the fence. On our return, the boat was cast off to catch the ebbing tide.

It was late when we arrived at the estuary of the river. We got off the boat and started walking home along the beach. It was dead at night; the sea was calm; the Casuarina groves stood uncharacteristically still; the far shadows of trees at the edge of the sandy expanse of the beach were motionless; the dark bluish mountains in the distant horizon had gone to sleep under a grey sky. When we reached home, my sleep drowned in depths, far deeper than sleep itself. The poem I wrote that night is intimately linked with the memory of a night from the past. Being unsure of what it would convey to its readers isolated from that memory, this poem was not published in the volume compiled by Mohit-babu. But I hope that if I give it a place in these memoirs, it would not be an unauthorised entry.

Hark I drown,
Deeper and deeper I drown,
Overwhelmed, benumbed, bemused.
Where, how far
At what hour of darkness
What path doth my mind choose?
O Mother Earth, beneath your feet
Pray, do not stop me,
O set me, set me free.
Unending days and nights
I go on drowning
Until, you are far, far from me.
You keep staring
Moonlight – the elixir of life,
Bewildered, fading stars in the sky;

O limitless horizon
Shelter me from above,
And spread both your wings up high.
No song, no words
No sound, no touch,
No sleep, no awakening flock –
Nothing wakes anywhere
Bathed all over with moonlight,
My entire being is benumbed in shock.
Limitless vacant sky
The world has floated away,
Nowhere to be seen –
In the middle of the night
Lonely and alone,
I know not to what unfathomable depths I've been!
Sing O world, you sing too
From distance unseen,
The sailor's song, sing
Millions sail with you
Where do you head for
I wonder eyes shut; what vision doth it bring?
Unending night
I sink, I'm snuffed out
I choke in the boundless nectar of the night
From one dot to another
Stirred and swirled,
I travel far and farther into the infinite.

It is essential I mention here, that when the mind is filled to the brim with some new feeling, it is not necessary that great writing will come out of it. The lines then get choked with emotion. Just as it does not work when imagination is totally separated from the person imagining, complete immediacy is also not unfavourable to writing poetry. The colour of poetry is best brought out by the brush strokes of memory. Reality can be oppressive – if it is not kept in check to an extent, imagination cannot find its place. Not only in poetry, but in every art, there must exist, aloofness in the artist – if the control is not in the hands of the creator within us, it will not work. If the subject overtakes the creator and tries to take control, then the result will be a mere reflection and not a portrait.

Nature's Revenge

IN KARWAR, I wrote a drama in verse titled *'Prakitir Pratisodh'*, or 'Nature's Revenge'. The protagonist is an ascetic who attempts to severe all bonds of affection and illusion, to win over the rules of nature, so that he could experience the infinite in its purest form. As though, the infinite existed beyond the reaches of reality. At last, a young girl succeeds in winning him over with her love and he comes back to this world, breaking his vow to unite with the infinite. Then the acetic realises – the great encompasses the small, the limitless includes the limited and in love there is salvation. When we are able to perceive in the light of love, we realise that even within boundaries, there are no limits.

The seashore of Karwar was such a place that made me realise that the beauty of nature is not merely a mirage in my mind; the joy of the limitless finds expression within this nature and we tend to lose ourselves in its beauty. Where the infinite expresses itself in the spell cast by nature outdoors, we may be unable to catch its glimpse concealed as it is within the regularity of natural phenomena; but where the heart inspired by beauty and love finds a touch of the supreme being within the smallest object lying right next to it – how can any argument work, faced with such perception? Nature led the ascetic along a path through his heart to the court of the infinite being, who ruled from the throne of the finite world. In *Prakitir Pratisodh,* on the one hand, there are people living along the path, the men and women of villages spending their ordinary days in building homes and raising families; and on the other, there is the ascetic who is trying his utmost to obliterate his home and everything else in the real world in his search for the infinite. When love bridges the differences between the two aspects, when a woman succeeds in winning over the ascetic, then in the union of the limitless and the defined, the false insignificance of the limited world and the false nothingness of the infinite disappear. Just as in my early life, I had entered an indefinably dark grotto within myself and lost my right over the world outside, and finally a beautiful bolt of light from the exterior world penetrated my heart and united me with nature – in *Prakitir Pratisodh,* I have attempted to narrate this experience in a slightly different manner. This is also a preamble to all my subsequent poetry. In fact, this is the sole underlying refrain in all of my poetry. This refrain can perhaps be titled, the song of finding the limitless within the realm of the limited. I expressed this very feeling in one of my later poems –

> The release, in the renunciation of the world, is not for me.

Among the essays compiled and published as 'Discussions' during this period, there was one where I attempted to describe the feelings inherent in *Prakitir Pratisodh*. I discussed limits that do not restrict, but try to reveal the unfathomable depths etched in a grain of sand. I do not know if this explanation has any value, or whether *Prakitir Pratisodh* can earn a place in the annals of poetry, but it is clear to me today that unconsciously, this singular idea has come to dominate my entire works.

On the way back from Karwar on a ship, I wrote a few songs of *Prakitir Pratisodh*. With great joy, I sat on the deck humming the tune as I wrote the lyrics of the first song –

> Beg you, O *Nandarani*,
> Let go of our *Shyam* –
> We cowherds are heading for the fields,
> Give us back our *Shyam*.

The sun has risen, the flowers are abloom, the cowherds lead their herds to graze – they do not wish to be alone in that sunrise, amidst those flowers, in the pleasure offered by the fields; they wish to be united with their *Shyam* at that very place, they long to see their Lord in the glorious dress of the infinite, in their midst; they want to be out in the fields, woods and hills, only to play with the infinite being who is also a cowherd among them; not sourced from afar, not in the realm of riches, their offerings are limited to garlands of wildflower anointed with sandal in decoration – since, if elaborate arrangements are made for the one whose limitless joy extends in all directions, there is every chance of losing focus.

A short while after my return from Karwar, on 8 December 1883, I was married at the age of twenty-two years.

Picture and Song

I WROTE MOST OF the poems, published under the title *'Chabi o Gaan'*, or 'Picture and Song', during this period.

We lived then in a mansion with a garden on Circular Road, near Chowringhee. A large community was located to the south of us. Very often, I sat beside a window on the second floor and looked out at the people of that community. I loved watching their myriad activities during the day, be it rest, play or simply coming and going – to me, their lives enfolded in a variety of tales.

I was possessed by a power of sight to observe everything around me. Then, I used to perceive seemingly independent scenes one by one in the light of my own imagination, and surround it with the joy in my mind. From among these, a special image or two caught my eye by the virtue of their essence or their colour. In this manner, I really enjoyed enhancing the pictures in my mind with my imagination. It was nothing more than a longing to draw a scene with the greatest clarity. It was a desire to perceive the objects in my mind with my eyes, and those beheld by my eyes with my mind. If only I could paint with a brush, then by line and colour, I would have tried to capture the frenzied vision and creation of my mind on a canvas, but my fingers lacked the skill. I only possessed words and rhythms. However, I had not yet learnt to draw clear lines with my words, and so the result was often a splash of colours. Just as a child gifted with a box of colours impatiently attempts to draw all sorts of pictures by every means available to him, so also after newly obtaining the box of colours of youth, I spent my days trying to draw a variety of pictures in my mind. If one correlates the age of twenty-two years with the pictures drawn during that period, then perhaps through their immature lines and blurred colour, it would be possible to get a glimpse of the artist.

I have written earlier that with *Prabhatsangeet*, a period of my life came to an end. With *Chabi o Gaan*, a new act commenced once again. The beginning of any endeavour is filled with excess. With progress, these get left behind on the wayside. At the beginning of this new act, I think there were several avoidable instances. If these were leaves of a tree, they would have surely fallen off. But the pages of a book do not fall off easily, they linger even after their days are over. This period of 'Picture and Song' marks the beginning of an act where even the simplest objects are perceived with much care. Just as the tune of a song can bestow deep meaning to the most ordinary lyrics, similarly in *Chabi o Gaan*, an attempt is apparent, to rid the mundaneness of a simple incident by dipping it in the spirit of the heart. No, it is not entirely that. When the strings of the mind are in tune, then a strain of universal music from any source can set it resonating. In those days, a tune was beginning to play in the writer's soul and it did not permit anything outside to be perceived as insignificant. On certain days, whatever I glanced at resonated within my heart. A small child can play happily with dust, sand, shells, snails or whatever pleases him, since the game is in his mind; he uses the joy of sport in his mind to truly discover the happiness in other games of the world, and finds satisfaction everywhere all around him; similarly, when the song of youth fills with myriad notes within our mind, then the resulting feeling enables us to realise that no place exists which is not tied to at least one of the millions of strings of the universal *veena* – then, whatever comes into view or into one's grasp, enlivens the concert within, without having to seek anything from afar.

The Child

BETWEEN THE VOLUMES *'Chabi o Gaan'*, and *'Kori o Kamal'*, or 'Cowrie and Lotus', a monthly magazine titled *'Balak'*, or 'The Child' flourished for a year as though enhanced by strong medicine, before its activities ceased forever.

Mejo-bouthakuran, or my third sister-in-law, was eager to bring out an illustrated publication for children. She wanted Sudhindra, Balendra and other boys of the household to write for the magazine. However, realising that a publication could not run on children's contributions alone, as a publisher, she requested me to share the burden. After an issue or two had been published, I travelled to Deogarh to see Rajnarayan-babu for a couple of days. While returning, the train was crowded at night and I could not sleep – there was a light directly over my eyes. I felt that since I could not sleep anyway let me take the opportunity to think of a plot for a story for the magazine. My futile attempts resulted in no plot, but sleep managed to steal across my brows. I dreamt that, seeing traces of blood from an animal sacrifice on the steps of a temple, a young girl is distressed and she implores her father, "Baba, what is this? Is it blood?" The father feels pain inside at his daughter's anxiety, but tries to suppress the question by feigning anger. I awoke and realised that, conceived in a dream, this could be the plot I was looking for. There are several other such instances where I dreamed up my story. I juxtaposed this dream with the legend surrounding the King of Tripura, Gobindamanikya and started serialising a long story titled *'Rajarshi'*, or 'The Ascetic King' in *Balak*.

Those were days free from any worries. Be it my own life, my prose or my poetry, nothing seemed to express itself intently to me. I had not yet joined the group of travellers but I sat in my room overlooking the road. People went by preoccupied with their own tasks; I looked on and the seasons - monsoon, autumn, spring stole in uninvited and spent their days in my room. But my business was not just with spring or autumn. There is no end to the list of strange people who came to visit me in that small room; they were like boats which had lost their anchors – they had no needs, they merely floated along. Among them there were a few wretches who came to me, deviously seeking to fulfil their schemes without any effort. But to fool me they needed no tricks at all – I was not worldly wise in the least and I failed to recognise deceit in any form. I paid for the education of many students for long, who needed no support and whose days of study were like vacations from the beginning to the end. Once, a long-haired youth brought me a letter from an imaginary sister. In it, she entrusted the bearer, her sibling, to my custody so that he could escape from the privations of a step-mother who turned out to be as much a figment of imagination as she was herself. Needless to say, I obtained definite proof that it was only the sibling who was not imaginary. Just as it is excessive to point a gun towards a bird that has not learnt to fly, the sister's letter seemed equally superfluous to me. In another instance, a youth came pleading that while he was studying for a B.A., his mental health was making it impossible for him to take the examinations. I was concerned, but since I was not an expert in medical sciences just as I had no expertise in any other field, I grew perplexed as to how I could reassure him in some way. He said, "I dreamt that in my earlier birth, your wife was my mother, and so if I could get to drink the water used to bathe her feet, I shall be cured." He paused, smiled a little and continued, "Perhaps you do not believe such things." I replied, "Does it matter if I do not believe – if it can cure you, so be it." And thus I handed him some water, feigning that it was what he desired. He drank the water and felt surprisingly better. Gradually and with ease, he progressed to having his meals under my roof. Thereafter, he took control over one corner of my room and called his friends over to smoke with him. Reluctantly, I left the smoke-filled room. Very soon, from several unpleasant incidents, it became clear that he might possess other ailments, but his mental health could not be doubted. After this, it became difficult even for me to believe persons claiming to be my children from a previous birth, without special proof. I realised that in this matter my fame had spread far and wide. One day, I received a letter about a daughter from my previous birth, who wished to receive grace from me as a cure for her ills. I was forced to draw a firm line here; my son had given me grief enough and I was not in a position to take on the responsibilities of supporting a daughter from my previous birth.

On the other hand, my friendship with Sri Sachandra Majumdar grew deeper. Quite regularly on evenings, he came to visit me along with Priya-babu. We sang and discussed literature until late at night. Some days too, were spent like this. Until a man's 'self' grows well-nourished and strong, his life floats by unchecked like autumn clouds and my condition was quite similar to that.

Bankimchandra

AROUND THIS TIME, I became acquainted with Bankim-babu. I first saw him many years ago. The old students of Calcutta University had just started an annual convention. Chandranath Bosu Mahasay was the chief organiser. Perhaps he envisaged that one day in the distant future, I too would find a place in the august assembly – and thus he invited me to the meeting to read some poem or the other. He was still in his youth. I can remember that he planned to read an English translation of a famous German war-poem, and in preparation, he rehearsed the lines by reciting them aloud in our house. The lines depicting the deep love of the warrior-hero towards his faithful follower - his sword in its scabbard that hung on his left - were the favourite of Chandranath-babu; from this fact, it is evident that not only was he possessed by extreme youth, but it was altogether a very different era.

While walking through the crowded gathering, among many different types of personalities, I suddenly spied one who stood out from the rest – there was no way of mistaking him for anyone else. I observed such a radiant glow on the face of that tall and fair gentleman, that I could not control my curiosity to learn his identity. Among all the various people assembled there, I asked only about him. When I got an answer that he was Bankim-babu, a sense of wonder was born in my mind. What struck me was, that the author whom I regarded to be great for his works, would also possess a definite mark of greatness in appearance. His sharp nose, his pursed lips and his penetrating gaze were the hallmarks of great strength. I noticed most of all, that with arms folded across his chest, he walked a path distinct from everyone else's, without mingling in the least with anyone. His expression was not merely that of an intelligent intellectual, his forehead was adorned with an invisible mark of royalty.

The memory of an incident which occurred at this stage is imprinted on my mind. In one room, a Sanskrit scholar was reading out *slokas* on nationalism that he had written, followed by his interpretation in Bengali. Bankim-babu entered and stood in a corner, listening. At one place in the poem, there was a rather crude, though not indecent metaphor. The moment the scholar began to amplify the expression in Bengali, Bankim-babu clasped a hand to his mouth and hurriedly exited from the room. I can still visualise that scene of Bankim-babu fleeing from the gathering.

Subsequently, I wanted to see him many times but did not get any occasion to do so. Finally, when he was the deputy magistrate of Howrah, I gathered up strength to go and visit him at home. I met him and tried my best to converse with him, but I came back feeling a little embarrassed. I felt that I had been rather immature in going to visit him uninvited, without proper introduction.

Since then I added a few years to my age; I was accorded a place as the youngest member among the writers of the time; but my position in the hierarchy had not yet been determined;

the little fame that gradually came my way was mixed with plenty of doubt and a lot of contempt; we, the writers of those days were each known by an English name, someone was Byron of Bengal, someone was Emerson, in this manner each had a certain given name; some people had started calling me Shelly – it was an insult to Shelly and a ridicule to me; I had earned the epithet of being a musical poet; then my knowledge was limited, my experience of life was inadequate, thus the prose and poetry I wrote had more imagination than substance, and, as a consequence, while these might have been considered good, there was no way to force praise from the readers. My dress and mannerisms were also a reflection of my partial flowering; I sported long hair and appeared to be in a poetic trance; I did not fit in, and could not conform to the most suitable prevalent common customs.

Around this time, Akshay Sarkar Mahasay started publishing a monthly titled '*Naba-jiban*', or 'A New Life' and I contributed a couple of articles.

Bankim-babu completed his stint with *Banga-darshan* and became immersed in religious discourses. A publication was started called '*Prachar*', or 'The Proclamation'. I contributed a song and an essay discussing the poetry of the *Vaishnava* sect.

Around this time or may be a little earlier, I gathered up strength and began calling on Bankim-babu once more. Then he was living on Bhabanicharan Dutta Street. I visited him alright, but there were no significant discussions to speak of. Mine was then the age to listen and not to speak. I hoped the conversation would pick up, but I hesitated to lead the charge. On some days, Sanjib-babu would be present, leaning against a bolster. I was pleased to see him since he was an approachable man. He delighted in conversing and it was a great pleasure to listen to his stories. All those who have read his essays must have noticed that he wrote with the joy and excitement of speaking aloud, as though he were carrying on a conversation in print; few people possess such power, and to be able to convey the spoken word in written pieces with the same degree of élan is rarer still.

During this period Sasadhar Tarkachudamani made his appearance in Kolkata. I heard about him first from Bankim-babu's lips. I think it was Bankim-babu who initially introduced him to everyone. At this time suddenly, the attempts by Hinduism to prove its superiority with the help of western science, gathered popularity in all directions. It was theosophy that had been spreading the banner of this revolution in our country for so long.

However, Bankim-babu did not join in this movement whole-heartedly. The shadow of Tarkachudamani did not fall on the explanations he presented on religious topics in his publication *Prachar*, since this was totally impossible.

I was then beginning to emerge from my corner and this was becoming apparent in my writing in the form of satirical poetry, comedies and letters to the newspaper '*Sanjibani*', or 'The Elixir'. I was able to break clear from the miasma of being overwhelmed by emotions and was beginning to rattle my sabre at the edge of the battlefield.

In the heat of the battle, I got into a confrontation with Bankim-babu also. The incident was chronicled in *Bharati* and *Prachar* of the day; there is no need to elaborate any further over here. In the end, Bankim-babu wrote me a letter which I have misplaced unfortunately – if it were here, readers could have seen how Bankim-babu successfully extracted the thorn of contention between us, with total forgiveness.

Ship's Hull

AFTER SEEING AN advertisement in the newspaper, Jyoti-dada headed off to the auctions one afternoon, and after his return, announced that he had purchased a ship's hull for a sum of seven thousand rupees. With the addition of an engine and superstructure, it was going to be turned into a proper ship.

Perhaps, he regretted that the people of our nation could work their pens, could work their tongues, but they could not work a ship. Once he had attempted to light up locally produced matches, but numerous strikes failed to produce a spark; he had been enthusiastic about running a domestic weaving mill, but the mill lay silent after delivering a single *gamcha* towel. And now he ended up purchasing an empty hull all of a sudden, in order to establish national shipping. One day, the hull filled up not only with an engine and cabins, but also with debt and misfortune. However, it must be remembered that all losses due to the attempt were personally borne by him while the gains must still exist, having accrued in the books of nationalism. All over the world, such unrestrained non-businessmen have been known to flood the economy of their nations with their unsuccessful ventures; these floods rise and then fall suddenly, but the layers of silt left behind give life to their respective nations – thereafter when the day of harvest arrives, no one remembers their names, but they who have borne losses all their lives, can easily accept this disappointment.

On one side there was the foreign shipping company, while on the other it was him alone – between the two parties, the intensity of the battle for supremacy in shipping commerce is surely remembered by the people of Khulna and Barisal to this day. Driven by competition, ship after ship was launched while losses mounted and earnings from the sale of tickets continued to diminish, but an age of bliss descended on the Barisal–Khulna steamer line. The passengers not only began travelling for free, they also availed free refreshments. Further, nationalist volunteers of Barisal set about collecting passengers by singing *swadesi kirtans* until the ships had no dearth of passengers, but all other sorts of shortages were on the rise. Nationalistic fervour cannot find means to enter the world of accounts; however entertaining the singing might have been, to whatever pitch the excitement might have risen, book-keeping could not forget its tables – therefore, three-times-three equals nine leapfrogged its way to ever-mounting debt.

Non-business like emotional men share the misfortune of being easily recognised for their frailty, while they fail to read other men; however, in order to learn of their inability to recognise people, they end up spending inordinate amounts of money and time, but are unable to use the lessons learnt to benefit in their present lifetimes. When the passengers were partaking in free refreshments, there was no indication that Jyoti-dada's employees were fasting like sages; thus, while free refreshments were arranged for the passengers, the employees were not deprived either, but the greatest gain of all accrued to Jyoti-dada for owning up to the all-encompassing loss of his entire fortune.

In those days, there was no end to our excitement in discussing the daily tally of victories and defeats in the Barisal–Khulna steamer line. Finally, news arrived one day that his ship *'Swadesi'*, or 'The Patriot' had sunk after striking the bridge near Habra. In this manner, when he had crossed all limits of his own capability and nothing else remained for him to show, it was then that his business truly folded up.

The Lament of Death

IN THE MEANWHILE, several deaths occurred in the family. Earlier, I had never observed death face to face. When my mother passed away, I was very young. She had been ailing for some time, but we had no inkling when it turned critical. So far, she slept on a separate bed in the same large bedroom as us. However, following her illness, she was taken on a cruise of the Ganges to recuperate, and upon her return, she lived in a third floor room of the inner chambers. On the night of her death, we were asleep; I do not know at what hour, an old maid of the family rushed into our room and burst out crying, "O what terrible misfortune has befallen you all!" Immediately, *bouthakurani* came in, rebuked the maid and led her out of the room, lest our minds suffer grievous harm. In the indistinct light of a dim lamp, for a moment my heart choked, but I just could not understand what had happened. In the morning, when I heard that my mother had passed away during the night, the words failed to register in my mind. I came out on the veranda and saw her bedecked still form lying on a cot in the courtyard. Her body displayed no evidence of the violence of death; the face of death that I beheld in the early light of day was one of peace and beauty of deep slumber. I failed to discern clearly between life and the end of life. It was only when her body was carried out through the front door and we followed the bearers on foot to the cremation ground, that grief struck like a sudden gust of wind which raised a lament in my mind that my mother would never again enter through this doorway, and take her seat in her own home where she had spent almost her entire life. The day lengthened, we came back from the cremation ground; at the turn of the lane, facing our house, I looked up at my father's room on the third floor – he was still seated in silent meditation on the veranda in front of his room.

The youngest daughter-in-law of the household was entrusted the responsibility of looking after the young children who had just lost their mother. She fed and clothed us and by keeping us close to herself, she tried day and night to make us forget the misfortune that had befallen us. One of the principal strengths of life lies in the power to forget the loss that cannot be compensated, the separation against which there exists no remedy; that strength is new and powerful during childhood, it does not allow any hurt to penetrate deep and make permanent imprints on the mind. Consequently, the first instance of death that entered our lives as a dark shadow was unable to leave behind a lasting darkness on us, and like a shadow, it departed on silent feet. Later on after growing up, on spring mornings, I used to tie a handful of half-opened buds of jasmine in one corner of the cloth covering my body and walk crazily around, rubbing the buds on my forehead every day to feel the smooth touch of my mother's gentle fingers; I could feel clearly that the beautiful touch that existed on the tips of her fingers were being reborn every day in the purity of the blossoms; she had no end in this world, whether we chose to remember or to forget.

However, my acquaintance with death at the age of twenty-four was of a far more permanent nature. This incident continues to connect and string together an extended garland of tears with every following incident involving sorrowful separation. The carefree life of childhood is able to run on ahead overtaking significant incidents of death with ease, but when one is older, there are no paths as easy to cheat death and move on with life. Thus, I had to bear the entire unbearable grief of that day on my shoulders.

I did not know then that gaps could exist in the fabric of the world; everywhere laughter and tears seemed to be woven tight. Nothing beyond was apparent and so I accepted this reality completely. Suddenly from nowhere, when death arrived to rend apart a portion of this closely held world in an instant, my mind was perplexed beyond measure. Trees and plants, earth and water, sun and moon, planets and stars existed with conspicuous fixity as before, but in their midst what had existed so far with equal certainty, the touch of the body, life, heart and mind of the person I had thought to be truer than all of these, dissolved like a dream in an instant; then looking out at the world, I was anguished at the strangeness of this self-contradiction. How was I ever going to unite what existed and what had ceased to do so.

Through this crack in life, an abysmal darkness appeared that pulled me day and night towards itself. I wandered and came to stop at the same spot, peering into the darkness, searching for what lay beyond. Humans cannot believe from within, in emptiness. What does not exist is false and whatever is false has no existence. As a result, our attempts to catch a glimpse of what is not visible, to lay our hands on the unobtainable, never seems to cease. Just as a plant enveloped in darkness tries its level best to balance on its toes and push upward to reach the world of light beyond, when death suddenly erected a fence of dark nothingness surrounding my mind, then my entire being endeavoured to emerge through it into the light of existence. No deeper sorrow exists than that experienced when the path through darkness cannot be discerned.

Even while burdened by unbearable sorrow, I was surprised when an unexpected zephyr of happiness stirred within my mind at certain moments. A load lifted off my mind even at the sad realisation that life is not unwaveringly certain. My mind rejoiced at the thought that we are not prisoners forever within the stone walled enclosure of reality. When I had to let go the person who was so close to me, its perception as a loss was deeply painful;

but considering it as a release, gave me much peace of mind. The all-encompassing overpowering encumbrance of the world, through multiplication and division of birth and death, regulated itself with ease from within and continued unabated; the realisation that this responsibility would not pin anyone down forever and no one needed to bear the oppression of living on in perpetuity as God, dawned on me for the first time that day like a new found truth.

Through that apathy, my mind was more deeply delighted by the beauty of nature. Since my deep love for life had disappeared totally for some days, the green profusion of trees and plants sheltered under a brilliant blue sky showered my teary vision with sublime sweetness. The separating distance required to perceive the world in all its completeness and beauty was created for me by the death in the family. I stood aloof, looked at the picture of the world in the vast canvas of death and realised that it was exceedingly beautiful.

For some time during this period, I was possessed by a weird emotion within, which manifested in equally strange behaviour outside. Holding social customs as infallible truth to be obeyed at all times, seemed a laughable practice to me. I could not be touched by such things. For some days, what the others thought did not bother me the least. Clad in a dhoti, a coarse piece of cloth over the upper body and a pair of sandals, I went over to Thackeray's house on many days to purchase books. My eating habits were also rather erratic. For some time, even during the rains and in winter, I had been sleeping out on the third floor veranda; from there I had a direct view of the sky above, and I could greet the breaking light of dawn without the slightest delay.

These were certainly not renunciation efforts towards a spiritual life. It was time for my vacation; the cane-wielding teacher of the world seemed like a downright cheat and in order to taste freedom, I began to evade the smallest rules set by the school. If I woke up one morning to discover that the gravitational pull of Earth had halved, why should I want to tread carefully on the government road? I would surely leap over the four and five storied buildings along Harrison Road for no reason at all, and while strolling on the *Maidan*, if the Ochterlony Monument were to come by, I would not be inclined to bypass it and walk past, but I would jump over it with ease and be on my way. I was then in such a state; the moment, the attraction of life reduced from beneath my feet, I almost gave up using paved roads.

Alone on the roof of our house, during the deep darkness of the night, I imagined a spire of the netherworld with a fluttering banner on top, and inscribed on the black stone of its main entrance there was a letter or a sign which I longed to see, and in the process, like a blind man, I groped about the entire night with both my hands. Then, at daybreak when the first light of dawn fell on my outdoor bed, I opened my eyes to see the veil wrapped around my mind become clearer; when the fog lifts, just as rivers, mountains and forests of Earth dazzle in brightness, my eyes beheld the picture of the living world to be fresh with dew and beautiful once again.

Monsoon and Autumn

IN SOME YEARS, a particular planet or two occupy positions of influence in the sky and this becomes apparent from the initial pages of the traditional almanac in the form of conversation between *Pasupati* or Lord Shiva and his consort, *Haimavati*. In the same manner, certain seasons take on special significance during certain phases of our lives. Looking back at my childhood, I remember rainy days most clearly. Rain driven by the force of the wind floods the veranda, the doors leading to the rooms are shut, our old maid Pyari is soaked to the skin as she hurries along the muddy pathway from the market with a basket laden with vegetables and I run the length of the long veranda driven by an immense joy. I can also remember going to school; our classroom was a part of a large covered courtyard partitioned by mats of woven bamboo strips; since early afternoon, stacks of dark clouds have been spreading across the sky; gradually the world is engulfed in thick sheets of rain; the sky resounds with extended peals of thunder; some crazed witch rends the sky apart with claws of lightning; gusts of wind threaten to knock down the partitions; it becomes difficult to see the printed letters of the book and *panditmosai* stops the lesson; seated on my bench, swinging my legs, I revel at the unexpected break from studies as my mind leaps beyond the raging storm outdoors and bounds along fields of imagination. I can further recollect late nights in the month of *Sraban*, the drumming of heavy raindrops permeates the gaps in my sleep and fills my consciousness with delight deeper than slumber; in half-awakened moments, I pray for unceasing rain into the morning so that when I awoke and looked outside, I could behold the lane leading to our house turned into a stream and the not a step at our pond's edge remained visible above the waterline.

However, in the period that I have reached in the course of my narration, autumn occupied the throne of my mind. The life of that period can be visualised in the wide clear sky of the month of *Ashwin* – in the molten gold like sunshine that pours over the dew laden bright green, I recollect that autumn morning, when I paced the south veranda, humming the lyrics I had composed in a tune set to *Raga Jogia* –

In a dreamy morn draped with the autumn sun
I know not what the mind longs for.

The day lengthens, the clock strikes the noon hour and without paying the slightest heed to pending chores, my mind rejoices in the passion of an afternoon tune, on another autumn day –

With careless ease the entire day,
What is this sport that overwhelms my mind?

I remember an afternoon lying sprawled on a carpet in the corner room, drawing in my sketch-book. It was not a rigorous exercise of art – it was a game to satisfy the urge to draw. What stayed behind in the mind and could not be sketched out was the important part. In the meanwhile, the golden hued intoxication of a lazy autumn afternoon poured in through the walls of an insignificant room in Kolkata and filled it to the brim. I do not know why it seems that the sky and the light which clothe the memory of those days are the same autumn sky and same autumn light of today. Just as it is the autumn that ripens the farmer's grains, it is also the autumn that ripens my songs; it is the autumn that fills the granary of my light-filled boundless leisure; it thrills my mind for no reason and it is the autumn which urges me to draw and write.

The difference between the monsoons of childhood and the autumn of my youth is that during the rains, nature engulfed me in a close embrace and with all its forces, decorations and musical instruments it accompanied me in a major concert. On the other hand, the primary celebration in the sweet brightness of autumn is human. With the interplay of the sun and the clouds in the background, a revolution of happiness and sorrow awakens, the colour of the blue sky is deepened by the passion of man's steadfast gaze and the wind blows notes of aspiration into the human heart.

My poetry now waits patiently at the doorsteps of humanity. There is no unrestrained access to the inside; there is hall after hall, doorway after doorway. Many a time one has to be satisfied with the mere glimpse of light inside; from within the doorway of the palace, strains of *Raga Bhairavi* played on the *shehnai,* reach the ears. Like spontaneous understanding of the mind with itself and compromise between desires, there are many other instances of give and take after overcoming crooked barriers. Thus, numerously obstructed, the torrent of life resoundingly dances along, flecked with the foam of laughter and tears, revolving in vortices at every step, until it becomes impossible to trace its path.

'*Cowrie o Kamal*', or 'Cowrie and Lotus' is the song of the abode of life, sung standing on the street in front. It is an entreaty for a place in the mysterious assembly –

I do not wish to depart from this beautiful Earth,
I want live on amidst all humanity.

This is the surrender of a tiny bit of life to the all-encompassing collective being.

Sriyukta Ashutosh Chaudhuri

WHEN I STARTED for England for the second time, I was acquainted with Ashu in the ship. He had acquired an M.A. degree from Calcutta University and was on his way to study law at Cambridge to become a barrister. We were together for the few days it took to sail from Kolkata to Madras. However, it turned out that the depth of acquaintance bears little relation to the count of days spent together. With easy compassion, he was able to win over my heart to such an extent, that the gap of unfamiliarity of not knowing each other earlier, filled up completely within the next few days.

After he returned from abroad, our relationship grew stronger. It was not yet the time for him to enter the business of law and lose himself in its depths. The crumpled money bags of his clients had not yet emerged to fill his coffers and he remained engrossed in seeking to collect honey from the forests of literature. I observed then that his being was overwhelmed by his feeling for literature. The literary breeze that blew from his mind lacked the whiff of morocco-bound volumes on library shelves. In that breeze, fragrances of flowers from unfamiliar gardens across the seas lingered and through our meetings, we seemed to go on picnics to some distant woods at springtime.

Ashutosh Chaudhuri had a special liking for French poetry. I was then writing the poems of *Cowrie o Kamal*. He observed resemblances between my poetry and those by certain French poets. He felt that many human feelings strongly attract the poet's mind and this fact finds expression in the poems of *Cowrie o Kamal* in myriad ways. The message in the poems is the unfulfilled desire in the poet's mind to seek entry into this life and to accept it to the fullest.

Ashu said, "I will organise these poems under appropriate chapters and publish them." He was entrusted with the task of publication. He chose the poem, 'I do not wish to depart from this beautiful Earth' to head the compilation. According to him, this poem contains the essence of the entire volume.

This is not impossible. During childhood when I was imprisoned indoors, I peeked through the gaps in the parapet on the roof of the inner chambers, looked at the unique Earth and reached out for it with all my heart. At the beginning of youth, human life attracted me with a similar force. I had no entry into its midst; I stood by at the edge and looked on. I raised the sails on my dinghy and was about to begin my voyage across the seas, when standing on the shore, my mind perhaps raised its arm to signal my helmsman. Life wanted to set sail in life's journey.

Cowrie o Kamal

IT WOULD NOT be right to say that I felt guilty for my unique social position where nothing stopped me from diving into the midst of life. In our country, there is little evidence to show that those at the centre of society are able to feel the tremendous force that drives life from all around. There are grassy banks around the pond and there is a *ghat* with steps leading down, while the cool shadows of ancient trees extend onto the dark waters; hidden in the thick foliage, the cuckoo calls out in a combination of the five primary notes – but this is a land-encompassed pond, where is the current, where are the waves and when is there ever a rush of the tide from the oceans? The free flow of human life cuts through rocky obstacles and in victory, wave after wave reaches the vast ocean; was the sound of this speeding torrent reaching my ears, from the community situated up my lane? No, this was not the case. An imprisoned soul cries out to be invited to the joyous or sorrowful occasions celebrating life.

In the mild inactivity that drives man to frequent midday siestas, life is deprived of its fullest capabilities, and thus he is surrounded by a lack of enthusiasm. I always felt pain at being entrapped in such a web of weariness and sought to break free. My mind refused to support the prevalent political meetings and newspaper revolutions that were bereft of self-confidence and also the semi-intoxication that possessed the educated of the day, caused by a nameless feeling for the nation without any spirit of service. A sense of dissatisfaction about myself and my surroundings enraged me and my heart cried – "If only I could be an Arab Bedouin!"

> At the arrival of the Goddess
> Joyous festivities spread across all lands –
> Behold, at the rich man's gate
> A poor lass; lonely she stands.

This tale is about me. In the communities where *shehnai* notes herald the festivities of the powerful and the independent, and where there is a ceaseless hubbub of people coming and going, we stand at the outer pavilion looking in with greedy eyes – did we ever get a chance to dress up and join in?

The painful aspiration, to experience life at large in all its variety within one's own, is only possible in a country as divided and as broken into segregated fragments as ours. Restrained indoors as a child, within a chalk marked boundary drawn by our servants, just as I longed for access into the free playground of the wide world, so also in the days of my youth, with a painful heart, I wished to reach out for the life force of the entire humanity. It was difficult to achieve, the path was untravelled and the goal was a distant dream. But if I remained unable to connect my life with it, if the winds did not blow in from over there, if the currents did not overwhelm, if travellers did not come and go, then the worn and aging would continue to obstruct the path of the new and if no one swept away the detritus of the past, it would also bury the living into obscurity.

The monsoon days are merely filled with dark clouds and rain. In the days of autumn, there is dalliance between the sun and the clouds but that does not cover the entire sky, and besides, crops ripen in the fields. Similarly in the monsoon period of my poetry, there was vapour, wind and pouring rain of outburst feelings. The rhythm then was uneven and the message was unclear. However, in the *Cowrie o Kamal* of autumn, no longer did the mere colours of the clouds in the sky dominate, there were also new crops on the ground. In keeping with reality, new words and verses attempted to grow by taking on diverse forms.

At last a period has ended. The days of intermingling in life between relations and strangers, and between the indoors and the outdoors are gradually becoming more cordial. From now on, life's journey will continue more along pathways on land, across habitation, traversing through good and bad as well as joy and sorrow and it can no longer be viewed lightly as a mere series of pictures. Now there will be much demolition and reconstruction, many victories and defeats, many conflicts and resolutions. Along obstructed, opposed and tortuous paths, with joyous dexterity, my life-preserving deity is leading me on towards flowering in an innermost endeavour and I lack the ability to reveal it with clarity. If I remain unsuccessful in bringing to light that astonishing and ultimate mystery, then whatever else I try to show will be mere misunderstanding at every step. The analysis of a sculpture yields its constituent mud and never the joy of creation of its sculptor. Thus, having arrived at the doorway to the inner palace, I will now take leave from the readers of my '*Jibansmriti*', or 'The Picture of My Early Life'.